Additional praise for W...

"Most business and data professionals struggle with delivering impactful presentations that consistently win the hearts and minds of their audience. In this book, Bill provides dozens of very practical and easy- to-adopt tips that will help you become an engaging and impactful presenter."

—**Mano Mannoochahr,**
Chief Data and Analytics Officer, Travelers Insurance

"Storytelling and data are both important, but extremely hard to bring together effectively. This book enables all readers with an interest in data to think about how to create and tell a story with data that engages, teaches, and informs both technical and executive audiences alike."

—**Eric Weber,**
Head of Data Product and Experimentation, Yelp

"Business communication has become critical in today's fast-moving world. In this book, Bill Franks has drawn on his many years of experience to create a simple guide with practical, readily usable examples that will help beginners in business communications develop effective skills, and help experienced practitioners remain on top of their game."

—**Dilip Krishna,**
Managing Director, Deloitte

"Whether you're a novice or experienced at presenting data, this book is packed with practical tips that will enhance how you approach your next presentation. Rather than taking years to learn these tips, like me, Bill Franks's sage advice will fast-track your ability to create and deliver impactful data presentations."

—**Brent Dykes,**
Author, *Effective Data Storytelling: How to Drive Change with Data, Narrative, and Visuals*, Founder/Chief Data Storyteller, AnalyticsHero, LLC

"The world is driven by data, and it is vital to understand how to use and apply analytics within your business. Bill Franks has written an excellent guide with 119 useful tips on how to become successful in presenting your data so it will have the most impact."

—**Dr Mark van Rijmenam,**
Author, *The Digital Speaker*, and founder of Datafloq

"Whether you are an internal or external analytics consultant, this book provides practical guidance for becoming an effective data storyteller. Highly recommended for data professionals at all levels."

—**Rod Bates,**
Managing Director, Data & Analytics,
PwC, and former VP, Decision Sciences and Data Strategy,
The Coca-Cola Company

"*Winning the Room* is relevant to a broad audience: The book is a pointed refresher for more seasoned business leaders, project managers, researchers, and consultants. It's also the one complete reference on presentation preparation for those early in their career: professionals, academics, and students alike."

—**Rasmus Wegener,**
Senior Partner, Bain & Company

"To achieve profoundly better data-driven presentations and communications, every presenter of data should study and learn from this book, and every data-related curriculum should require this book for all their students. The book is a well-ordered guide through a full menu of must-dos, don't-dos, how-tos, and why-dos in data communications, data presentation, data storytelling, and presentation design."

—**Kirk Borne,**
Chief Science Officer, DataPrime.ai

Winning the Room

Winning the Room

Creating and Delivering an Effective Data-Driven Presentation

BILL FRANKS

WILEY

Published by John Wiley & Sons, Inc., Hoboken, New Jersey.
Published simultaneously in Canada.

For general information on our other products and services or for technical support, please contact our Customer Care Department within the United States at (800) 762-2974, outside the United States at (317) 572-3993 or fax (317) 572-4002.

Wiley also publishes its books in a variety of electronic formats. Some content that appears in print may not be available in electronic formats. For more information about Wiley products, visit our web site at www.wiley.com.

Library of Congress Cataloging-in-Publication Data

Names: Franks, Bill, 1968- author.
Title: Winning the room : creating and delivering an effective data-driven
    presentation / Bill Franks.
Description: Hoboken, New Jersey : Wiley, [2022] | Includes index.
Identifiers: LCCN 2021046310 (print) | LCCN 2021046311 (ebook) | ISBN
    9781119823094 (paperback) | ISBN 9781119823131 (adobe pdf) | ISBN
    9781119823100 (epub)
Subjects: LCSH: Business presentations. | Business—Data processing.
Classification: LCC HF5718.22 .F73 2022 (print) | LCC HF5718.22 (ebook) |
    DDC 658.4/52—dc23
LC record available at https://lccn.loc.gov/2021046310
LC ebook record available at https://lccn.loc.gov/2021046311

Cover image(s): © Getty Images | Klaus Vedfelt
Cover design: Paul McCarthy

SKY10032357_010722

*This book is dedicated to everyone
who is fully committed to making the effort required
to deliver effective data-driven presentations.*

Contents

Foreword   xvii

Preface   xxi

Acknowledgments   xxv

About the Book   xxvii

Intended Audience   xxxi

Overview of the Contents   xxxiii

**SECTION 1   PLANNING: REVIEWING STRATEGIC
                FUNDAMENTALS**   1

TIP 1:   Results Are Not the Biggest Factor in Success   3

TIP 2:   Data Literacy Is a Two-Way Street   5

TIP 3:   Don't Write Your Story . . . Tell Your Story!   7

TIP 4:   Facts and Figures Are Not a Story   10

TIP 5:   Know Your Audience   12

TIP 6:   Slides Must Be Short, Visual, and to the Point   14

TIP 7:   Charts and Graphs Are Like Jokes   16

TIP 8:   Short Presentations Are Harder to Prepare
                Than Long Ones   18

TIP 9:   An Executive Presentation May Have No Slides at All   20

TIP 10:   Budget Appropriate Time   22

TIP 11:   Be Yourself and Be Authentic   23

TIP 12:   What Is the Audience Buying Into? You!   24

SECTION 2   PLANNING: DESIGNING THE PRESENTATION   25

TIP 13:   Different Presentation Venues Require Different
                Approaches   27

TIP 14:   Try Different Ways to Organize Your Story   29

TIP 15:   Too Many Technical Details Will Undercut Your Impact   31

TIP 16:   Reveal Details Only to the Extent Required   33

TIP 17:   Focus on How to Use Your Results   35

TIP 18:   Use Analogies to Make an Impact   37

TIP 19:   Make Liberal Use of Appendices   38

TIP 20:   Create a Distinct Leave-Behind Document   40

TIP 21:   Create "Launch" Slides   43

TIP 22:   Break Content into Smaller Pieces   45

TIP 23:   Animations Are Your Friend   48

TIP 24:   Action Settings: A Hidden Gem   50

TIP 25:   Show the Fewest Numbers Necessary   52

TIP 26:   Distinguish Technical Significance from Business
              Significance   54

TIP 27:   Give the Audience Your Headlines   56

TIP 28:   Start with Your Recommended Actions   58

TIP 29:   Don't Focus on the "What"   60

SECTION 3   DEVELOPING: WORDING AND TEXT   63

TIP 30:   Minimize the Number of Words on Your Slides   65

TIP 31:   Use Simple Terms and Definitions   67

TIP 32:   Don't Use Technical Terms   69

TIP 33:   Clarify Your Definitions   70

TIP 34:   Provide Layperson and System Labels   72

TIP 35:   Use Consistent Phrasing   74

TIP 36:   If It Can't Be Read, Don't Display It   76

TIP 37:   Don't Shrink Your Font, Shorten Your Text   78

TIP 38:   Use Appropriate Spacing   80

TIP 39:   Use the Same Font throughout Your Presentation   82

TIP 40:   Beware the Missing Font   85

TIP 41:   Address Every Agenda Item Listed   87

TIP 42:   Identify When an Agenda Item Is Covered   89

TIP 43:   Spellcheck Is Not Always Your Friend   91

TIP 44:   Charts and Images Are Misspelling Factories   93

TIP 45:   Beware the Right Word, Wrong Place   94

TIP 46:   Keep Your Text Horizontal   95

SECTION 4   DEVELOPING: NUMBERS AND LABELS   97

TIP 47:   Use Consistent Precision   99

TIP 48:   Use Only the Precision Required to Make Your Point   101

TIP 49:   Match Precision to Accuracy Level   103

TIP 50:   Always Format Numbers   105

TIP 51:   Always Show Percentages as a Percentage   108

TIP 52:   Provide Quantities *and* Percentages   110

TIP 53:   Never Use Scientific Notation   112

TIP 54:   Use Names, Not Numbers, for Categories   114

TIP 55: Watch for Truncated Labels   116

TIP 56: Define All Acronyms and Abbreviations   118

TIP 57: Use Dedicated Definitions Slides   120

TIP 58: Clarify Aggregations Applied   122

TIP 59: Focus on the Outcome of Interest   124

TIP 60: Validate That Your Numbers Make Sense   126

TIP 61: Add a Scale to Every Chart   128

TIP 62: Ensure Your Charts Have Consistent Scaling   130

TIP 63: An Axis Usually Should Start at 0   132

TIP 64: Number Your Slides   134

SECTION 5   **DEVELOPING: CHARTS, IMAGES, AND LAYOUTS**   135

TIP 65: Use a Mix of Chart Types   137

TIP 66: Use a Mix of Slide Layouts   139

TIP 67: Do Not Show Raw Output   142

TIP 68: Keep It Simple   145

TIP 69: Choose Charts That Are Easy to Interpret   147

TIP 70: Don't Show Incomprehensible Graphics   149

TIP 71:   Use Complex Graphics Strategically   151

TIP 72:   Coordinate Your Colors   153

TIP 73:   Keep Colors in Context   155

TIP 74:   Shun Technical and Architectural Diagrams   157

TIP 75:   Don't Let Accent Graphics Steal the Show   159

TIP 76:   Format Tables Consistently   161

TIP 77:   Use Shading to Make Tables Easily Readable   163

TIP 78:   Don't Put Borders Around Charts   165

TIP 79:   Limit the Number of Categories   167

TIP 80:   Label Your Data   169

TIP 81:   Avoid Stacked Bar Charts   171

TIP 82:   Put the Cause on the *X*-Axis   173

SECTION 6   **DELIVERING: FINAL PRESENTATION**
                PREPARATION   175

TIP 83:   Practice Your Presentation   177

TIP 84:   Consult Some Confidants   179

TIP 85:   Don't Overprepare   181

TIP 86:   Adjust Your Story to the Audience   182

TIP 87:   Focus on Time, Not Slide Counts   185

TIP 88:   Always Be Prepared for a Short Presentation   187

TIP 89:   The Audience Won't Know What You Left Out   190

TIP 90:   Scale Figures to Be Relatable   192

TIP 91:   Be Clear about the Implications of Your Results   194

TIP 92:   Call Out Any Ethical Concerns   196

TIP 93:   Use Simplified Illustrations   198

TIP 94:   Don't Include Low-Value Information   200

TIP 95:   Make Critical Numbers Stand Out   202

TIP 96:   Make Important Text Stand Out Too   204

TIP 97:   Have Support in the Room   206

TIP 98:   Always Have Several Backup Plans   207

TIP 99:   Use a Slide Clicker   209

TIP 100:   Do Not Send Your Presentation in Advance   210

SECTION 7   DELIVERING: GIVING THE PRESENTATION   213

TIP 101:   Do Not Read Your Slides . . . Ever!   215

TIP 102:   Read the Room and Adapt   217

TIP 103:   Do Not Look at the Screen!   219

TIP 104:   Physically Point to Important Information   221

TIP 105: Don't Let Bright Lights Throw You Off   222

TIP 106: Don't Stand Still   223

TIP 107: When Presenting Online, Look Right at the Camera   225

TIP 108: Anticipate Random and Irrelevant Questions   227

TIP 109: Handle Difficult People with Grace   228

TIP 110: Don't Correct People in Front of the Room   230

TIP 111: Never Pretend You Know If You Don't!   232

TIP 112: Stress the Positive   234

TIP 113: Be Honest about Costs as Well as Benefits   236

TIP 114: Don't Hedge Too Much   239

TIP 115: Be Clear about the Measure You Are Discussing   241

TIP 116: Don't Ask Which Findings Are Important   242

TIP 117: Tie Facts to Impacts   243

TIP 118: Provide Specific Recommendations for Action   245

TIP 119: Close with a "Wow" Tied to the Larger Context   247

Afterword   249

About the Author   251

About the Website   253

Index   255

Foreword

How to deliver effective presentations—there's a topic that's frequently written about. And it should be! Effective communications, particularly in boardroom, client, conference, and other stakeholder presentations, is an essential component of success in business and in one's personal career development. What's new and urgent now is the need for *data-driven* communications. How one presents and communicates raw numbers, derived results, and inferred actionable insights from data are essential leadership and career skills in the current data-drenched digital era.

To be honest, my very first reaction when Bill asked me to write a foreword was "Oh, no, not another 'How to deliver effective presentations' book!" But then, the emphasis on live, in-person data presentation, data communication, and data storytelling (with a sprinkling of fun examples within my favorite category, "how to lie with graphs and statistics") made me quickly get drawn in and fully engaged with the book.

Bill's narratives are anchored solidly to specific tips with corresponding specific graphics. It quickly becomes clear that he has lived through the good and bad examples provided. I also loved the rationales Bill gives, answering the "why" when he recommends a way to do something. This makes every page a real learning experience for the reader. I ended up thinking to myself, "Here's a case where first impressions were wrong." And it was a delightful experience to have my mind changed in such a positive direction.

Data literacy is a very commonly discussed soft skill that goes along with data storytelling for effective data communications. What is important about any communications is that its success is measured in two ways—in the one communicating and in the recipient. Simply adequate data communications could be achieved by a data-literate speaker presenting things clearly enough but without showing empathy with the audience through good data storytelling. Conversely, good storytelling is lost on the audience if the speaker does a poor job in explaining the numbers and the insights derived therefrom. In the first case, the presenter engages with the data but not with the audience. In the latter case, the audience is engaged with the story but not with the data.

Ideal data communications therefore succeeds both ways, with the presenter and the audience in synch. In synch with what? In synch with understanding the answers to the three data-driven questions that should be addressed in the presentation: What? So what? And now what? In other words, What did I do and what did I learn from the data? Why should you care? And what data-driven actions should you now take?

To achieve profoundly better, even perfect, data-driven presentations and communications, every presenter of data should study and learn from this book, and every data-related curriculum should require this book for all their students. The book is filled with brilliant tips, spanning more than 100 nuggets of data-driven wisdom, from a master data analytics practitioner, business consultant, storyteller, and thought leader. You will find here a well-ordered guide through a full menu of must-dos, don't-dos, how-tos, and why-dos in data communications, data presentation, data storytelling, and presentation design.

The book's ultimate strategic goal is clearly stated in the first part of its title: *Winning the Room*. Backed up by years of experience and his own stories, Bill delivers a wealth of practical advice and recommendations that delightfully satisfy the tactical objectives of the book: "Creating and delivering an effective data-driven presentation." Proven in the hard-won trenches of client engagement, the positive reinforcement checklist style of the book will be a refreshing departure from those preachy books that tell you what you are doing wrong in your presentations. This book delivers, page after page, on the promise of helping you to learn the how and why of *Winning the Room*.

Kirk Borne, PhD, Chief Science Officer, DataPrime.ai

Preface

You're part of a high-performing team that has some great data-driven results to share. After months of effort, the team's work on a major project is finished and you're ready to present the results to the senior leaders in your organization. You and the entire team are energized and excited about the upcoming presentation and spend substantial time pulling together the necessary facts and figures. Those facts and figures are impressive and leave you no doubt that what your team has found will yield massive benefits for the organization once the executives act on the findings. As you step to the front of the room, turn on your laptop, and start your data-driven presentation for the audience, you're feeling confident and proud.

The first information presented is a list of the key milestones of the project. To make sure that you accurately summarize the milestones, you turn to read the dates and descriptions from the screen. As you discuss the project's methodology, you provide the technical details behind each phase so that the executives understand the extent of the work your team did. You don't want the presentation to appear too long, so you keep your slide count to a minimum by putting as many points as possible on each slide. As the presentation progresses, questions indicate that audience members aren't understanding the technical details, so you go over all the details again, frustrated that they don't understand such simple concepts.

In preparing the presentation, you reused many of the technical slides that were used to explain the results to the extended project team because the slides had been proven effective with that audience. You notice a few spelling and grammar errors early in the presentation but figure that nobody else will notice before you fix them. All numbers in the presentation are shown to three decimal places to reinforce the rigorous precision the team practiced, yet an audience member identifies some numbers that are not correct. You promise to update the figures before distributing the presentation.

At the end of the presentation, you summarize the facts the project team uncovered and the data that supports those facts. The executives ask questions to better understand the business and practical context of the results and how to make use of the information properly, so you promise to add more information on those topics before distributing the presentation. After asking the audience what they find most compelling about the findings, you are stunned at the lack of excitement exhibited by the executives. To help move things forward, you state that your primary recommendation is for the executives to reconvene to discuss what actions they might take based on the findings. You conclude by saying that you and the project team look forward to hearing what potential actions the executives identify and which they decide to pursue first.

After the team's months of hard work, no actions are taken, and the project is shelved. You receive feedback that the executives found the presentation hard to understand, unfocused, and boring. They certainly didn't see the potential you and your team saw. Worse, as far as the stakeholders are concerned, you and your team are now associated with an embarrassing failure of a project. Bye-bye end-of-year bonus! You are baffled by this and soon leave the company to find a job at an organization with executives who will be more enlightened and appreciative of your hard work.

Unfortunately, the same pattern repeats at the new company, and every company after that, because the problem wasn't with the executives in the audience . . . it was with you.

There were many errors in the presentation delivery described in the preceding paragraphs. I hope you noticed many of them. If not, don't worry because this book is here to educate you on what went wrong and what to do differently. Delivering an effective data-driven presentation to a(n) (often nontechnical) live audience isn't the same as discussing technical details with peers. Entirely different ways of organizing and presenting information are necessary to help an audience that doesn't have your expertise to do the following:

- Understand what you've found.
- Grasp the implications.
- Take action.

Delivering a live presentation is also very different from compiling a written document. You must be purposeful and diligent if you want to develop a presentation that conveys a compelling story while simultaneously avoiding myriad traps that undercut your credibility and limit your impact.

If your goal is to create and deliver effective data-driven presentations, this book will explain how to do that!

Acknowledgments

There are many individuals who get credit for helping to make this book happen. First are all the clients and coworkers over the years whom I presented to and watched present. Without delivering and watching so many presentations, I would not have had the opportunity to learn the lessons contained in this book.

I owe huge thanks to the students in the 2020–2021 Data Science 7900 classes I helped teach at Kennesaw State University. Seeing the struggles class members had with the early versions of their project presentations drove home in my mind how much there is to learn about developing presentations. The classes helped reinforce the need for some of these tips through their efforts. More important, seeing how fast the classes improved as they learned from their errors gave me the confidence that a book like this could have immediate impact for readers and was worth writing.

I also owe thanks to Jennifer Priestley and Sherill Hayes for being supportive and encouraging of this project. Their input helped to solidify the book's strategy and direction.

Finally, thanks to the people who were kind enough to review and provide feedback on my initial draft of the book. The input I received led to many changes and much rearranging that made the book better. Thank you to Fraser Douglas, Bill Franks (my dad, not me!), Mike Lampa, Scott Langfeldt, and Krista Sykes.

About the Book

Data literacy is one of the hottest topics in the business world today. Although most people think of literacy in terms of reading and receiving information, literacy is a two-way street that also involves writing and delivering information. The presentation of data-driven material is, therefore, a core component of data literacy. The onus isn't just on your audience to be ready to understand and receive the information you provide. The responsibility is also on you to present and explain your information in a way that can be effectively received by your audience. You must also help the audience understand what they stand to gain by acting on the information.

This book focuses on common errors that presenters make when delivering a data-driven presentation to a live audience. The negative effects of these errors are only magnified when presenting to nontechnical audiences, and the errors drastically undercut the impact of your presentation while lessening your personal credibility. Although presenting information in a clear, crisp, effective fashion enables you to stand out, it takes diligence and practice to do that consistently.

In the context of this book, a *data-driven presentation* is one that contains summarized data, analysis results, survey outcomes, results of experiments, or any other type of data derived to support the presentation. Also note that *presentation* in context of this book applies to a slide deck prepared for a live presentation and to how the presenter verbally delivers the compelling story that the deck supports. The live presentation can be in person, virtual, or a mix of both.

Although many of the tips in the book also apply to written content, the book is all about making live data-driven presentations. There are many books on different aspects of delivering data-driven content, such as performing analysis, creating visualizations, storytelling, presentation skills, and more. However, this is the only book that pulls from each of those subject areas and applies a lens focusing exclusively on the live presentation of data-driven content.

The tips that follow are derived from my 30+ years of presenting data-driven information to mostly nontechnical audiences. I have delivered hundreds and hundreds of presentations to companies and conferences myself, and I have been present in a similar number of presentations by others. Every tip in this book reflects a mistake that I have made and/or that I have seen others make. Ironically, some of the mistakes that seem so obvious as to make you say, "I'd never do that, so why did it get included in this book?" are the mistakes I see most often! I've always wished someone had taught me these lessons so that I didn't have to learn them the hard way on my own, hence, my motivation to write this book and provide the lessons to readers as a way to pay it forward.

This book is needed now more than ever. Analytics and data continue to rise in prominence, and virtually anyone in the professional workforce today must deal with data, as a presenter and as a consumer of presentations. Although universities teach the theory behind how to generate analytics and data, they do not spend time on how to effectively present that information to others. Most continuing education and corporate training courses are similarly focused on generating technical results, not effectively delivering those results to an audience. Due to this, people still learn what they know about how to present data-driven information on the job, and, frankly, most people aren't very good at it! If you learn to present data-driven information well, you will increase your effectiveness, your credibility, your career success, and the number of business outcomes you influence.

This book is meant to be a handbook that you keep on your desk so that you can refer to it on an ongoing basis during presentation development. Just like athletes continue to practice basic skills throughout their careers, it is also necessary to constantly refresh yourself on how to create and deliver data-driven information effectively and to routinely practice the basics.

Intended Audience

Although the book uses many examples from the analytics and data science space, because that is my background, the concepts are valid for anyone presenting results that include technical information and data. Businesspeople, engineers, chemists, professors, doctors, sociologists, students, researchers, and others who create and deliver data-driven presentations will all benefit from the book because the tips can be applied quite broadly.

For experienced presenters who are good at what they do, the book will be a terrific refresher and handbook. There will almost certainly be tips that even experienced presenters either didn't know or often forget to practice.

For people newer to presenting data-driven information, the book will be an invaluable guide that will help you avoid learning the same lessons through the experience of making the mistakes yourself.

In an academic setting, professors can assign the book as support material for capstone classes or applied study programs that require delivery of project work.

In a team setting, giving difficult feedback to teammates is easier and less personal if you can say "It says in this book to do it this way" as opposed to "I don't think you should do it that way."

By reading the book and then keeping it handy as a reference, readers of all experience levels and roles will greatly enhance the effectiveness of their own data-driven presentations.

Overview of the Contents

This book contains nearly 120 specific tips with nearly 150 illustrations that are arranged in sections that flow from planning a presentation, to developing it, to delivering it. Each tip is short and to the point, often with accompanying illustrations, so that any tip can be read and absorbed in just a few minutes. Although some tips relate to similar underlying concepts, each will stand on its own, so you can read any tip in isolation and apply it. Because tips stand alone, there is also no need to read the book sequentially and, if desired, you can focus on sections where you feel you need the most help.

By following these tips, you'll get better at creating and delivering presentations that provide information in a manner enabling it to be received, understood, and embraced by your audience. This combination will help increase the level of data literacy within your organization while increasing your influence. Each section is described briefly here.

Section 1: Planning: Reviewing Strategic Fundamentals

Regardless of the audience or topic, there are core strategic principles that underlie any successful live data-driven presentation. This section covers fundamental presentation concepts that you should review and account for as you design, develop, and deliver your presentation. After all, doing a great job with the details discussed in later sections of the book won't make up for having a foundational presentation approach and strategy that is poor.

Section 2: Planning: Designing the Presentation

Before creating any slides, you must take the time to design your presentation. It is necessary to determine the story you want to tell, the order in which you'll introduce information, the level of depth you'll cover, what you want the audience to remember, and what actions you want the audience to take. Moviemakers don't simply start shooting scenes and then hope to chain them together after the fact into a good movie. Rather, they design the overall story and each scene in immense detail before any filming takes place. You must follow this model to create and deliver an effective data-driven presentation.

Section 3: Developing: Wording and Text

The text that you place on your slides and how that text is worded are critically important to audience comprehension. You must get your points across clearly and succinctly while using terms and phrases that your (often nontechnical) audience can understand. Perhaps the simplest rule of thumb is to always read the content you develop through the lens of the intended audience. If the person in your organization who is least knowledgeable about your topic would be able to read and understand your points, then you are on the right path.

Section 4: Developing: Numbers and Labels

Numbers will be front and center during any data-driven presentation and so you must make those numbers friendly to your audience. The tips in this section enable the numbers that you show to convey the message you intend while minimizing the effort required for your audience to consume and interpret the information. How you label and format your numbers will have a significant impact on how your presentation looks and how well it is understood by your audience.

Section 5: Developing: Charts, Images, and Layouts

The charts, tables, and imagery you incorporate into your data-driven presentation and how you lay them out within your slides will have a large impact on your audience's perception of your presentation. Thus, it is well worth the effort to carefully consider what visuals to use, how to format them, and how to arrange them on your slides. You cannot take raw output and drop it into your presentation. You must create charts, tables, and imagery that effectively communicate the information you want to convey. The tips in this section help your presentation look great while successfully communicating your core messages to the audience.

Section 6: Delivering: Final Presentation Preparation

After you've developed your presentation content, you must prepare for and practice your delivery. Knowing what you'll say, anticipating the questions you'll receive, and validating that your spoken words flow smoothly are critical to success. Your final preparation is the last chance to ensure your messaging is on target, your slides are easy to follow, and that you're able to successfully drive home the points that you want to make. During final preparations, you'll always find some fine tuning that will make your presentation better as well as spots where you realize that you need to make your verbiage clearer and crisper.

Section 7: Delivering: Giving the Presentation

When the big day has arrived and you're stepping to the front of the room, there are still a range of things to focus on if you want your presentation to be a success. This section will cover various presentation mechanics to use, as well as some important principles to follow, as you deliver your data-driven presentation. If you win the trust and confidence of the audience, you can motivate them to embrace your conclusions and act on your recommendations. This, in turn, will enable your efforts to be a resounding success!

Section 5: Developing Charts, Images, and Graphs

Section 6: Delivery: Final Presentation Preparation

Section 7: Delivering/Giving the Presentation

Planning: Reviewing Strategic Fundamentals

Regardless of the audience or topic, there are core strategic principles that underlie any successful, live data-driven presentation. This section covers fundamental presentation concepts that you should review and account for as you design, develop, and deliver your presentation. Here are some of the concepts discussed in this section:

- Realize that your presentation is at least as important as the work behind it.
- Understand your audience.
- Recognize your responsibility to make your material accessible to the audience.
- Embrace the need to tell a story, not just present facts.
- Be yourself and earn the trust and confidence of your audience.

The tips in this section will support the presentation creation and delivery process that follows. After all, doing a great job with the details discussed in later sections of the book won't make up for having a foundational presentation approach and strategy that is poor.

Tip 1: Results Are Not the Biggest Factor in Success

The most important factor in determining if a given project will succeed or fail in a business environment is *not* the quality of the results. In an ideal world, that would be the case, but it isn't true in the real world. Using analytics as an example, let's discuss why your presentation is *at least* as important as the results.

First, let's be clear that producing accurate results is crucially important. Every professional creating any type of analytical output must ensure that results are valid and accurate every time. However, from the viewpoint of project sponsors, the results themselves are *at most* 50% of the criteria that will determine if they view the project a success.

At least 50% of the success of a project will be based on how well the results are put together in a presentation, how that presentation is delivered, and how the results are perceived by the audience. The presenter must be able to explain the results in a way that makes sense to the audience and convinces them of the value so that they will be comfortable taking action. Success isn't just about focusing on finding the right results, however tempting that may be. Success also requires taking time to focus on the right interpretation, positioning, and presentation of the results to the (usually nontechnical) sponsors who asked for the project to be executed.

A nontechnical stakeholder won't care about the weeks of effort and the gory details of getting to the results. They care about what the results mean to them and their business. If you fail to get the results across to your audience effectively, the results may as well not exist. In other words, producing great results is *necessary, but not sufficient,* to have the project viewed as a success.

Given that the impact of mass advertising is very hard to quantify, why has it maintained a huge share of marketing expenditures? In part, it is due to the advertising industry's ability to make what they do compelling to their sponsors through a great story. Advertising agencies fully understand and leverage the power of presentation and emotion when they make their pitches to their clients. Imagine how successful an analysis can be if highly measurable actions based on solid analytics are paired with the excitement level that advertising pitches instill in their sponsors!

In many ways, making a complex analysis accessible to the audience can be harder than the analysis itself. It takes hard work, multiple iterations, and deliberate practice to develop the ability to distill a lengthy and complex set of results down to digestible sound bites. At times, you may feel you are watering things down too much and focusing on "fluffy" slides instead of "meaty" algorithms. Although it is necessary to have the details behind the findings available, the details shouldn't be brought out unless necessary (see Tips 15 and 16). A nontechnical audience's eyes will glaze over, they'll tune out, and they won't act on the results if your presentation gets too technical.

Your mission is to present results in a way that keeps the sponsors engaged and interested. You must accept the need to stop doing more analysis in favor of readying yourself to successfully present what you've done. Never forget that producing great results is necessary, but not sufficient, to having a project viewed as a success!

Note: This tip is based on content from Chapter 8 of my book *Taming the Big Data Tidal Wave* (Wiley, 2012).

Tip 2: Data Literacy Is a Two-Way Street

As discussed in the Preface, data literacy is one of the hottest topics in the business world as I write this. According to Dictonary.com, literacy is "The quality or state of being literate, especially the ability to read *and* write." The emphasis on the word *and* is my own and is done to highlight a common gap in the understanding of what literacy is. Specifically, most people tend to think of literacy as being about effectively reading and receiving information. People often forget that literacy is a two-way street that also involves effectively writing and delivering information.

Recognizing that literacy is a two-way street is critical if you want to deliver a successful data-driven presentation that effectively conveys the information and implications that you desire to convey. If your audience isn't understanding you, don't automatically assume that it is their problem that they aren't able to properly consume the information. It is also quite possible that you are delivering the information poorly. To achieve data literacy requires that you successfully write, speak, and convey the information while the audience simultaneously reads, hears, and receives the information correctly.

A big part of the job of a publisher like Wiley (the publisher of this book) is to provide editors who ensure that what an author writes is grammatically correct and comprehensible. Publishers focus on the writing side of literacy. We rarely see poorly written information that has been formally published in a book because of this editing process. However, you can likely think of occasions when you saw a personal blog someone posted that contained good ideas but was so poorly written that it was hard to understand what the author was getting at.

As you develop and prepare your presentation, take your side of literacy seriously. Make sure that you're viewing your content through the lens of those you will be speaking to (see Tip 5). Don't include terms or acronyms without defining them (see Tip 33). Have another person review your material and provide feedback just like an editor at a publishing house (see Tip 84).

The critical point to remember is that the onus isn't just on your audience to be ready to understand and receive the information in your presentation. The responsibility is equally on you to present and explain the information in a way that can be effectively received by your audience! Both sides of literacy must be present if you want to succeed.

> *Note:* This tip is based on my blog *Struggling with Data Literacy? That's Great News!* (International Institute For Analytics, December 2020).

Tip 3: Don't Write Your Story . . . Tell Your Story!

When presenting technical results, it is your opportunity to tell a compelling story that informs the audience of the key facts and figures they need to know while also engaging and motivating them toward action. Your slides should serve only as visual backup for your main points. During the presentation all eyes and attention should be focused on you as you tell your story (we'll define more clearly what a story is in this context in Tip 4). There is plenty of time for people to read through the details. That time is specifically *not* during your presentation.

Many technical people make a major error when developing a data-driven presentation. Namely, they fail to distinguish between a detailed, written document and a visual, live presentation that tells a compelling story. A written document can (and often should) contain detailed backup data to support the points being made, and it can also include information that requires time and focus for the reader to absorb it. A live presentation needs to keep content as simple as possible. It is common to develop what is effectively a detailed written document and then present it live. The problem with that approach is that your audience will try to read everything on the slide while you are talking, which will make them miss much of what you are saying and miss the context you provide.

The slide in Figure 3a looks like many you have seen before. In fact, I have seen slides that are even worse! The slide is text-dense and hard to read. It would not look nice even as a handout. When projected on a screen during a presentation it looks ridiculous and destroys your credibility. Many presenters compound the error of including such a slide by then more or less reading what is on the slide (see Tip 101). That only makes the situation worse and bores the audience.

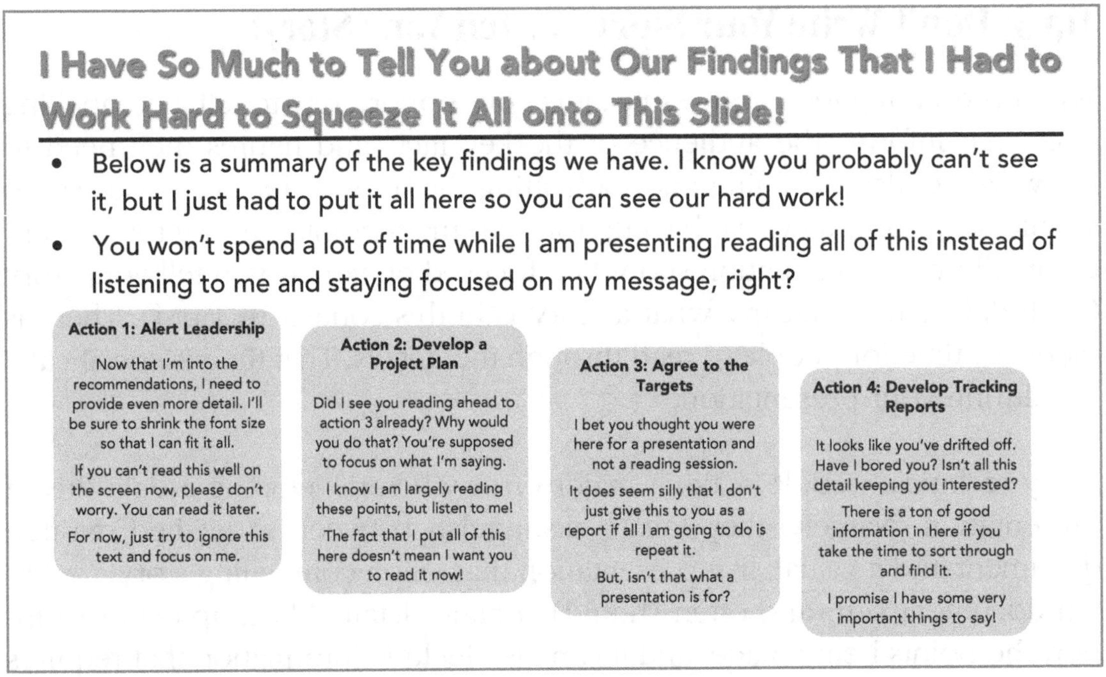

I Have So Much to Tell You about Our Findings That I Had to Work Hard to Squeeze It All onto This Slide!

- Below is a summary of the key findings we have. I know you probably can't see it, but I just had to put it all here so you can see our hard work!

- You won't spend a lot of time while I am presenting reading all of this instead of listening to me and staying focused on my message, right?

Action 1: Alert Leadership

Now that I'm into the recommendations, I need to provide even more detail. I'll be sure to shrink the font size so that I can fit it all.

If you can't read this well on the screen now, please don't worry. You can read it later.

For now, just try to ignore this text and focus on me.

Action 2: Develop a Project Plan

Did I see you reading ahead to action 3 already? Why would you do that? You're supposed to focus on what I'm saying.

I know I am largely reading these points, but listen to me!

The fact that I put all of this here doesn't mean I want you to read it now!

Action 3: Agree to the Targets

I bet you thought you were here for a presentation and not a reading session.

It does seem silly that I don't just give this to you as a report if all I am going to do is repeat it.

But, isn't that what a presentation is for?

Action 4: Develop Tracking Reports

It looks like you've drifted off. Have I bored you? Isn't all this detail keeping you interested?

There is a ton of good information in here if you take the time to sort through and find it.

I promise I have some very important things to say!

FIGURE 3A An Example of Too Much Text

Detail at the level in Figure 3a might be okay if it is being sent via email for someone to read on their own without a verbal explanation (though the specific format of Figure 3a is horrible for any purpose!). After all, people eventually need to understand the details and context along with the main points. However, such a slide will doom a live presentation and your story will not be heard even if you successfully tell it. The audience will either be reading your slide and ignoring you or tuning out because they find the slide overwhelming.

Although it takes more work, it is important to set aside your lengthy leave-behind document and create a shortened, visual version to use for your live presentation. The presentation should provide just enough information to highlight the key points you will be discussing in your story.

The Analysis Proved Our Approach Works

We recommend four actions based on the results

**Alert
Leadership**

**Develop a
Project Plan**

**Agree to the
Targets**

**Develop Tracking
Reports**

FIGURE 3B A Cleaner Approach

The slide in Figure 3b has only the most salient points and it can be presented using animations (see Tip 23) so that only one of the items is revealed at a time. The audience will read each point almost instantly and then shift focus back to you. During the presentation, you can add as much commentary as needed, but you'll do it verbally as you tell your story instead of showing your story in writing and then talking over it.

Tip 4: Facts and Figures Are Not a Story

We'll talk a lot in the book about keeping your audience focused on your story. But what exactly is a story? It is more than just facts and figures. Facts and figures are the main characters and the focal points of your story. However, you can't simply recite the facts and figures to achieve success. You'll also need to explain how those facts and figures relate to each other and what they imply for the problem you're attempting to solve. Most important, you'll need to help the audience understand why the findings matter to them personally and what actions they should take as a result of the findings.

That last point is what your story is all about. Facts and figures by themselves can be interesting to technical people, but especially for a nontechnical audience, pure facts and figures won't get the job done. It is on you as a presenter to make those dry facts and figures interesting and compelling to the audience. There are entire books on storytelling, so we can't do the topic full justice in one tip. For our purposes, we'll focus on a few cornerstones of developing a story.

First, you can't tell a story until you've created a story. The initial step is to decide what your story is. This entails identifying what it is about your findings that will matter most to the audience and how that information can be provided in a way that resonates with the audience's way of thinking and helps them understand what actions they can take to achieve their own goals.

Start by laying out your key facts and findings, how they relate to each other, and what actions they imply. Then define the important takeaways you want the audience to remember and the actions you want them to take. Last, develop a cohesive verbal narrative that makes the totality of the information accessible and compelling to your audience. Emphasize how what you've found will have an impact on a wider constituency than just those in the room by providing visibility to broader benefits. For example, if you're presenting a way to make a supply chain more efficient, don't just talk about the direct savings to the supply chain organization itself (though you must discuss that). Also discuss how the small businesses you work with will have to deal with less product spoilage and how customers will experience fewer out of stocks.

You must also present a vision of what will happen after the actions you suggest are implemented. Paint that vision using phrases such as "Imagine when we can . . ." or "It is exciting to think that we may soon be able to . . . ." Don't approach this as a cheesy, used-car sales exercise. Rather, focus on enabling the audience to see the bigger vision your results support and not just the tactical steps you're recommending today.

Whatever you do, don't be the stereotypical technical presenter who provides only facts and figures and then is surprised that the audience isn't excited and motivated to take action. Without some anecdotes, some humor, and some help understanding the bigger vision, the audience will hear nothing more than a recitation of boring data. What a nontechnical audience really wants, and what you must deliver, is a story they are happy to pass along to others and to act on with enthusiasm!

Tip 5: Know Your Audience

One of the best ways to set yourself up for success and to lower the chance of missing the mark is to research your audience. You should do your research up-front before you start putting together your presentation and laying out your story. This is because what you learn about the audience can greatly affect the approach you must take with your presentation and what content and narrative will be most appropriate. If you wait until your presentation is done and it is almost time to present, then you may not have time to make the necessary adjustments for your audience.

What should you learn about your audience? As much as you can, of course. Specifically, here are a few core pieces of intelligence you should try to gather:

- What goals does the audience have that your presentation can help them meet?
  - In a business setting there is no better way to get someone on board than to show them how your work will help them earn their bonus!
- What needs does the audience have for information or support?
  - If your audience is desperate for more information on how to solve a critical problem and you can help, you'll be their new best friend.
- What are the main priorities of the audience as it relates to your work?
  - If your audience has a top priority to cut costs, you might position your findings differently than if the top priority is to grow revenue or to increase customer engagement.
- How interactive is the audience?
  - In some organizations, people are very quiet and mainly listen. In others, they'll jump in early and often. That affects your timing and flow. Know what to expect.
- Is the audience predisposed to embrace or resist your findings?
  - Depending on if your news is viewed as good or bad, the goals and priorities attendees have, and political realities, the audience will come in with very different attitudes.

The ideal method for gathering this information is to find a confidant within the team you're presenting to who can help you with much of the intelligence just discussed. In my consulting work, we'd always try to find the "coach" within the client's team who was on our side and would help us understand the realities inside the organization. (More on this in Tip 84.) Of course, if you've worked with your audience in the past, you should already know the personalities and politics.

Although you'd love to have everything aligned in your favor, this is rare. Now and then you might have to present findings that don't help the audience reach their goals and don't address their top priorities . . . all while the politics of the day make them resistant from the start. That's a tough audience! In that situation, plan to do a good presentation, earn the audience's respect and trust for the future, and don't let it get to you when your recommendations are not implemented. Sometimes, you must play your role in the game even when you're in a losing situation. Most audiences will respect when someone delivers a no-win presentation professionally.

Your primary goal is to know what the audience wants and where they stand and then to maximize the impact of your presentation in context of that knowledge. Although you won't win every time you present, you will score more points every time by being prepared with an understanding of your audience.

Tip 6: Slides Must Be Short, Visual, and to the Point

A primary way to make your data-driven presentations more effective is to keep each slide short, visual, and to the point. Force yourself to narrow each slide down to the essence of what you want to communicate. This is very difficult, and it takes practice, but it will pay off big . . . especially with nontechnical audiences. With visual slides, audiences will better focus on the story you are telling, which will make them more likely to comprehend your main points and will make your presentation more likely to be successful.

Equally important, the audience will come to think of you as one of those rare technical people they like interacting with because they are able to understand you and you seem to understand them. Nontechnical audiences often enter a presentation by a technical person assuming (whether fair or not) that they will be bored and confused by technical jargon.

In Tip 3 we talked about telling your story, not writing it. You want people focused on what you are saying . . . and everything on the screen is a distraction from that. The more that's shown on the screen, the more the audience will focus their attention on the screen. Naturally, if the audience is busy reading and interpreting what's on the screen, they are specifically *not* listening to what you are saying.

It will feel to you as an expert that your slides aren't complete and aren't providing everything the audience needs to know. That is true, intentional, and desirable! You are there to provide the rest of the content and context through your verbal commentary. Your slides simply help guide the flow of the discussion. One way to keep slides simple is to lay them out simply as shown in Figure 6a.

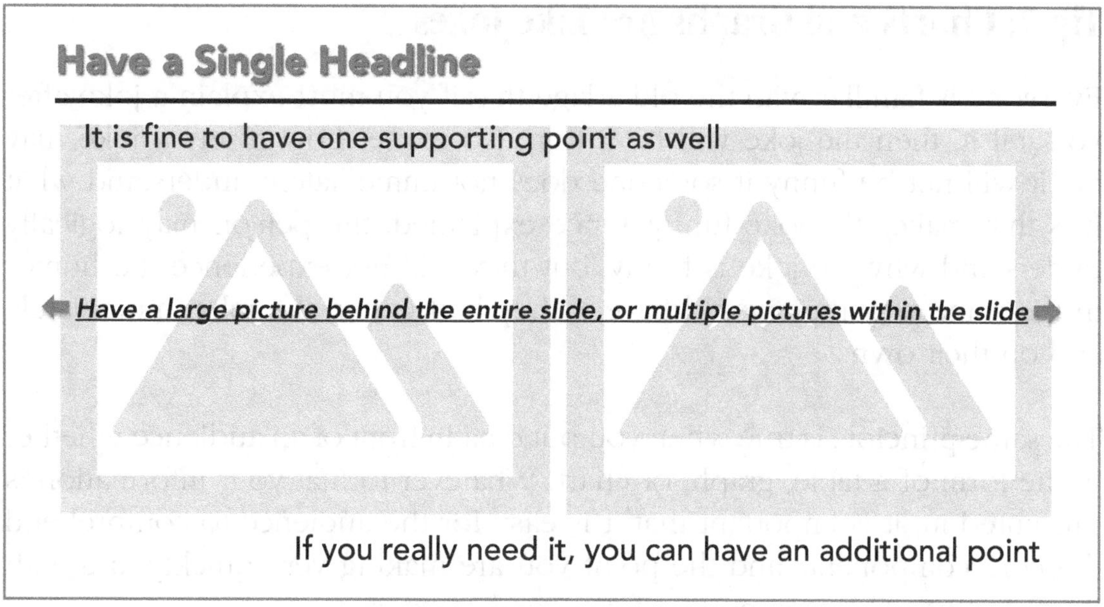

Have a Single Headline

It is fine to have one supporting point as well

← *Have a large picture behind the entire slide, or multiple pictures within the slide* →

If you really need it, you can have an additional point

FIGURE 6A A Clean and Visual Layout

Tip 7: Charts and Graphs Are Like Jokes

Everyone is familiar with the old adage that if you must explain a joke after you tell it, then the joke will be a flop. No matter how funny a joke may be, it will not be funny if someone does not immediately understand what it is that makes the joke funny. Once explained, the person may logically understand why the joke is funny, but they will not experience the humor in the same way they would have if they had gotten the joke immediately and on their own.

The same principle is true when you put data in front of an audience whether in the form of a table, graph, or chart. Whatever format your information is presented in, it is important that it is easy for the audience to comprehend the core components and the point you are making very quickly and with limited effort. This is important for several reasons:

- Per Tip 3, when you are presenting, you want people listening to you and the story you are telling. You do not want them struggling to understand the data projected on the screen.
- The more an audience struggles to understand what you are showing them, the more they lose interest and the lower your credibility goes. People trust experts whom they understand and who they believe understand them.
- People walk away impressed and thinking highly of a presentation if the information provided was clear and easy to comprehend. Technical experts have a reputation for being hard to understand, so if you can surprise the audience by making things simple, you will have a win.

Throughout this book, many tips are provided to help you keep your presentation as simple and understandable as possible. Always force yourself to look at what you have drafted through the eyes of the audience for which it is intended (see Tips 5 and 86). What may seem obvious and basic to you as an expert may not be perceived the same way by an audience that lacks your expertise and experience.

In summary, just like with a joke, if you must explain your chart or graph for people to get the point, then you have failed. People will not go see a comedian a second time if many of the comedian's jokes are hard to understand because that takes the fun out of the show. Similarly, if you spend a lot of time explaining your charts and graphs, the audience will not be inclined to come to another presentation of yours. As an aside, another way that charts and graphs are like jokes is that most are bad. Many Tips in this book will help you avoid making bad charts and graphs!

Note: This tip was the basis for my blog *Charts and Graphs Are Like Jokes* (International Institute for Analytics, May 2021).

Tip 8: Short Presentations Are Harder to Prepare Than Long Ones

Often, people get concerned when they are asked to give a long presentation. In my experience, a lengthy presentation isn't usually a problem because of these reasons:

- It is easy to make all of your points even if you ramble on more than is necessary.
- You aren't forced to substantively focus and trim your presentation.
- If your points aren't clear, there is time to answer audience questions to clarify your points.
- If you make a mistake or get sidetracked by the audience, there is plenty of time to recover.
- If you end a long presentation early, that leaves time for discussion and/ or gives the audience some time back. You win in both cases!

However, preparing a short presentation is very difficult because of these reasons:

- There is no time to waste, so you must be focused and crisp.
- You are forced to trim your material to a minimum.
- It may not be possible to cover some points at all, which requires prioritization (see Tip 89).
- You must rehearse to make sure you will stay within your time limit (see Tips 83 and 87).
- The audience must understand your story easily because there is no time for clarification.

I have put together literally hundreds of presentations and I can say without question that the hardest presentations are the shortest ones. When a conference says I have 45–60 minutes, I know it will be easy to hit the mark. When I have 30–35 minutes, I know I'll need to do some trimming and focus my story. When I have 20 minutes, which is getting more common in recent times, my blood pressure immediately spikes because I know that I will have to really work hard to make my talk compelling.

A short presentation requires you to get right to the point, with little context, and with little time to defend your points. The story you tell must be brief, easy to understand, and impactful. This is quite hard to do. Short presentations are the ones you should worry about, so don't make the mistake of assuming they will be easy and neglect to budget sufficient time to develop your presentation (see Tip 10) and to practice your delivery.

Tip 9: An Executive Presentation May Have No Slides at All

As you move up the organizational chart to higher-level audiences, the best way to deliver your presentation changes. To the extent you do show slides to a senior executive, the slides must be even more high level and strategic in nature than you would use for the executive's team. Executives want to quickly understand the business impacts and outcomes along with the associated risks and costs, make a decision, and move on.

For very senior audiences, I recommend that you consider not using any slides at all. Executives get inundated with presentations every day and they are tired of slide after slide of information in meeting after meeting. I have found that the energy level of a senior audience visibly rises if I start the presentation by saying, "We have some slides we'll leave behind for you, but I thought we could just talk through the key points." Executives usually love the idea of getting to actually *interact* with someone rather than listen to yet another person *talk at* them. You must have your story down pat and you have to be comfortable going off script, but if you can pull off a slide-free discussion you will stand out to a senior audience.

Going slide-free does not mean you haven't prepared your presentation, however. Keep your slides in front of you printed out like in Figure 9a (the same format is discussed in more detail in Tip 88) so that you can still follow your planned flow. If you put the printout in your notepad, the executives won't notice and you can take notes while simultaneously looking at the slides. You'll be "presenting" your story and following along with your slides in your mind even though they aren't displayed. As you cover a slide, you can check it off so that you can track what points you still need to hit.

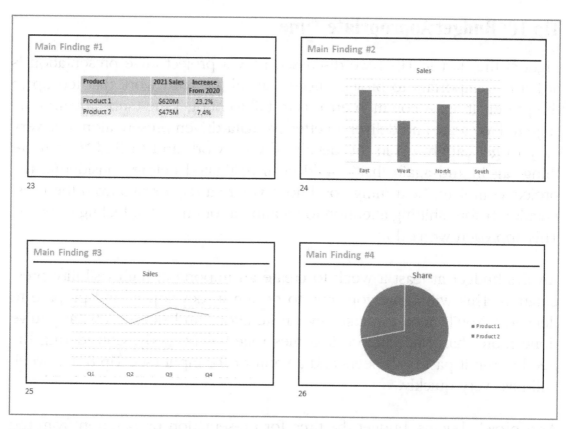

FIGURE 9A Go Slide-Free with Printed Slide Snapshots

An additional advantage is that as time winds down, if you have a few points that you haven't been able to make yet, you can say, "Before we run out of time, I'd like to make a couple of final points." Then you can proceed to finish off your story and ensure that you've delivered the message you intended to deliver, albeit in a slide-free manner. If you have to leave some less important points out, that's okay as long as you hit the most important ones (see Tip 89). This is an approach that can lead the executive(s) to be ready to take action.

Tip 10: Budget Appropriate Time

Right at the start in Tip 1 we discussed how a project's live presentation is at least as important to project success as all the hard work that led up to the presentation. A common error is to fail to budget the (substantial!) time required to create and deliver an effective data-driven presentation. It is very easy to get caught up in the details of your work and to find "one more thing" again and again that should be investigated before considering the project complete. Next thing you know, you're a day or two from the presentation before shifting attention to creating it, often with a feeling of panic. This approach won't do.

Always budget at least a week to create an important, high-visibility presentation. This will allow you time to design it, develop it, and prepare to deliver it. You'll need to make several iterations and sleep on what you've done more than once before it comes together properly. Considering the need to run it past both peers and a sponsor for input (see Tip 84), a week will pass very quickly.

As a project begins, budget the time for presentation preparation from the start. Back up the due date for the results at least a week, if not two, to build in the time necessary for presentation development. It is also possible to split duties so that some people are trying to improve the findings while others are putting together the presentation. Dropping in updated numbers isn't hard to do once you have the slides laid out and the presentation drafted. For smaller projects, you might not need a week, but it is still important to budget a realistic amount of time relative to the size of the scope.

Tip 11: Be Yourself and Be Authentic

The tips in this book will help you improve your data-driven presentation and storytelling skills. However, don't take any of them to the extreme and lose your authenticity. Audiences like people who seem genuine, comfortable, and authentic. If you force yourself to speak or act in a way you would not usually do, the audience will notice it and it will hurt your credibility and limit your impact.

Advice abounds about terms to use, terms not to use, and the latest hot phrases and buzzwords. But no matter how perfect your terms and how current your buzzwords, if it clearly isn't "you" who is saying them, then they will fall flat. It is better to be authentic and say something in a slightly awkward fashion than to recite a perfect phrase in a robotic, monotone voice.

You know how you typically phrase things, the speed you usually speak, and how much hand gesturing is natural for you. Unless you receive repeated negative feedback that something in your natural style is distracting, then don't change your natural style. I often technically violate common "rules." However, I often get positive feedback on those violations because people like that I'm just being myself.

I once sat through a presentation skills course led by a very nice instructor who really tried to practice what she preached. However, she took it to such an extreme that it came across as totally inauthentic and forced. She stood straight and stiff in front of the room. When she made a series of points, she would very clearly say "One," "two," "three" while holding her hand at just the right height with her fingers showing the number with perfectly spaced precision. What she was doing was technically correct, but totally removed her personality and style from the mix. It was inauthentic.

Don't let your presentation style drift toward something ineffective and distracting, but don't try so hard that your true self is lost either. Be yourself. Be self-aware. Monitor the audience's mood and reaction (see Tip 102). Embrace your own presentation style. But always be authentic.

Tip 12: What Is the Audience Buying Into? You!

With all the time the book focuses on what goes into your presentation and how to deliver it, it can be easy to forget that *you* are a primary component of an effective data-driven presentation. Regardless of the facts, format, or style of your presentation, it will be successful only if you build the trust and credibility necessary for your audience to understand, accept, and then act on what you have presented.

An award-winning presentation delivered well by someone whom the audience doesn't like or trust will fail. It is better to deliver a mediocre presentation while winning the trust of the audience than to deliver a pretty presentation without winning trust. However, you need to strive for a solid presentation *and* the winning of audience trust.

A good presentation itself builds trust because it shows you cared enough to do a good job and it gives the audience the information they need to remember. Typically, every stakeholder won't attend every presentation. As a result, good collateral also helps impress those who miss a live performance when they see the content later.

Your takeaway from this tip is that your audience, particularly if they are nontechnical, will be buying into *you*, not just your content. They want to trust that you handled the technical details, solved their problem, and will help them succeed in their goals. No matter how big and impressive a team you belong to, during your presentation the audience is deciding if they trust you as an individual. The success of your efforts hinges on getting them to decide that they do trust you and that they want to act on your findings. Don't forget this as you proceed through the presentation-focused tips in the book.

Planning: Designing the Presentation

Before creating any slides, you must take the time to design your presentation. It is necessary to determine the story you want to tell, the order in which you'll introduce information, the level of depth you'll cover, what you want the audience to remember, and what actions you want the audience to take. You'll also need to plan how to verbally convey all of that information.

If you learn to be disciplined about taking the time to design your presentations, you'll soon realize not only how much better and more effective your presentations are but also that the time spent in the design phase is far less than the time wasted on revisions to a presentation that wasn't properly designed up-front. Here are some of the concepts discussed in this section:

- Identify the type of presentation that you need for each situation.
- Determine how much detail to include.
- Make use of approaches, such as animations and appendices, to streamline a presentation.
- Keep practical implications front and center.
- Focus on what the audience should do with the results more than what you did to generate the results.

Moviemakers don't simply start shooting scenes without a plan or script and then hope to chain them together after the fact into a good movie. Rather, they design the overall story and each scene in immense detail before any filming takes place. You must follow this model to create and deliver an effective data-driven presentation.

Tip 13: Different Presentation Venues Require Different Approaches

Most of the tips in this book apply to almost any situation. However, some are more (or less) critical depending on the venue for your presentation. Here we'll consider three distinct venues for a data-driven presentation: a business venue, a conference venue, and an academic venue. Each has nuances and adjustments that you will need to make if you want your presentation to be a success.

Business presentations are where I have seen the most mistakes made over the years. This is unfortunate because the stakes are often high in a business setting. Everything in this book applies to a business presentation. Business presentations often must cater to a wide diversity of backgrounds and technical abilities in the room. It is also quite common that the very people you most need to influence have the background least like yours. It should go without saying that it is critical to apply the tips from this book in a business setting.

Conference presentations require some adjustment. One advantage is that your audience will typically be more consistent in background based on the choice to attend a given conference. It is unlikely that non-accountants will attend an accounting conference, for example. Although the audience may be able to handle a little more technical detail due to its familiarity with your topic, they can also be a tough audience in that they'll expect to learn some genuinely new things from you.

One challenge at a conference is that you usually cannot discuss the specific impacts or recommendations that help solidify a business presentation because you are presenting in public and must respect confidentiality. The visual appeal of your slides will be even more important in a conference setting if you want to stand out from the sea of presenters. You are also much more likely to be driven to your appendices during the question-and-answer period because the audience will typically desire to and be able to dive deeper into your topic.

Academic presentations can be a different animal altogether. I believe that all of the tips aimed at clarity, readability, and visual appeal apply fully in an academic setting. Unfortunately, very few academics agree based on the presentations I've seen! Most specifically, in an academic presentation you often must make what would otherwise be a technical appendix a core part of your presentation. An academic audience will often expect the gory details and will want you to go through them.

With that said, the academics I know who have been successful in developing a strong reputation do follow the principles in this book. It is part of what helps them get noticed. It also helps them appeal to audiences broader than just those deeply involved in their core discipline. Especially if you're new to the academic world and need to build your reputation and win tenure, you need to do what you can to stand out. The tips in this book are one way to do that.

To summarize, regardless of the presentation venue and audience, you'll be wise to make use of the tips in this book. Some tips are more or less important in different settings, but none can be ignored. You will always benefit from telling an engaging, entertaining, and compelling story while making use of visually appealing, clear, and straightforward slides.

Tip 14: Try Different Ways to Organize Your Story

Although starting with your key findings and recommendations (see Tip 28) and closing with a call to action (see Tip 118) are almost always the way to go, there is a lot of leeway in how to organize the arguments in between. There are occasions when the order in which to present the various supporting facts is clear-cut. Usually, however, there will be many options which all seem reasonable. How do you decide how to organize your presentation for the biggest impact?

Order your content in a few different ways. This doesn't take long. Simply list the key points and arrange them in different ways to represent the options you find worth considering. To illustrate, see Figures 14a and 14b, which show two options for ordering points. Creating each flow was as easy as dragging the slides around. You want to start and end strong. To do so, be sure to put some of the most compelling points up-front and in back. Particularly contentious or controversial points will need to be handled with care. Place them early or late depending on the culture and practices of your specific audience.

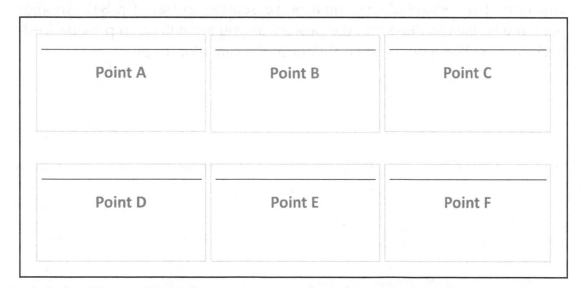

FIGURE 14A Story Flow 1

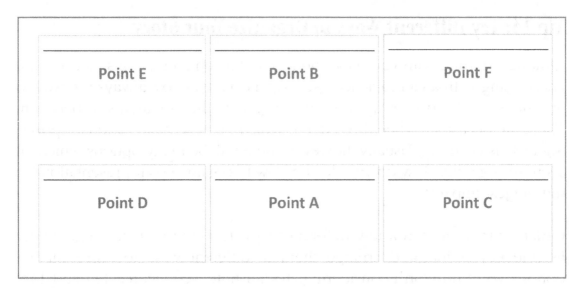

FIGURE 14B Story Flow 2

Once you've generated some options, put them aside for a while and then come back later with fresh eyes and review them again. Likely, you'll quickly note a couple orderings that flow better than the others. Once you've decided on an option or two that you like best, run them past a colleague and, ide-ally, one of the stakeholders you'll be presenting to (see Tip 84). Another person who isn't as deep into the process as you are will often provide feed-back that enables you to be confident in the direction to go.

Tip 15: Too Many Technical Details Will Undercut Your Impact

It is appealing to think that helping an (often nontechnical) audience understand the details of our technical efforts would increase our credibility and impact. Unfortunately, it doesn't work that way. Suppose you visit two local auto mechanics to help with a broken-down car. Which of these two mechanics would you give your trust and business to?

Mechanic 1:

"It looks like you have a transmission issue. I'll need to run multiple tests to validate that including a fluid test, an electronics test, and an internal diagnostics test. Let me explain those tests to you." (five minutes of painful technical detail on each test)

"Depending on what the tests find, I may or may not be able to fix it quickly. One less common scenario I've seen with these symptoms requires an entire new transmission, which would cost several thousand dollars and take about two weeks. While that scenario is possible, it isn't probable."

"We're also having issues with our primary supplier right now. I don't expect we'll have an issue with transmission parts, but I just wanted to alert you that we won't know for sure until we place the order. I can give you a firm time and cost estimate tomorrow I hope, depending on if my sick mechanic gets back to work. Should I check the car in?"

Mechanic 2:

"This is almost certainly a transmission issue. Most likely with these symptoms I can fix it in three days for about $1,500. Although I can't commit to that until we take a look, I'll be able to give a firm commitment within 48 hours. Should I check the car in?"

Although mechanic 1 provided much more detail and technical background about the tests, risks, and range of outcomes, you'd likely leave that discussion feeling uneasy and overwhelmed. He told you much more than you needed or wanted to know. Most people wouldn't choose to leave a car with him. Mechanic 2 was concise and confident. He acknowledged that there were risks, but he stated what he thought the issue was and was very clear on the path to completion. Most people would leave that discussion feeling much more comfortable than with the first even though they were provided much less detail.

People come to you as an expert to handle the technical details they don't understand. They want *you* to worry about the technical details; they don't want you to teach them the technical details. So, what does your audience want from you?

- A summary of your results
- An understanding of what the results imply for them
- Specific actions they can take as a result

You must be credible, and you must communicate well to deliver that wish list to your audience. But never forget that they are trusting you as the expert to handle the technical details. Helping them understand what they can do to address their problems given what you've done will lead to a successful project and further requests for support in the future.

Note: Based on my blog *A Common Trap That Undermines Analytics Credibility* (International Institute for Analytics, February 2019).

Tip 16: Reveal Details Only to the Extent Required

Although you don't want to volunteer too much detail (see Tip 15), it is important to properly gauge exactly how much to reveal when someone does ask for details. Although executives and nontechnical audience members rarely want to know technical details, there are always exceptions where you are asked to dive deeper. That raises the question of how much detail to reveal. Follow these three rules:

- Go into technical details only if explicitly asked to do so.
- Provide the minimal level of detail required to satisfy the person asking . . . and no more.
- If only one person seems interested in the topic, suggest a follow-up one-on-one so that you can avoid taking the room in a direction most don't want to go.

The reality is that most people asking you to tackle a technical endeavor won't care about the details and only want confidence that you can handle their problem. They have come to you, much like you'd go to a mechanic (see Tip 15), because they are assuming that you have the knowledge that they lack to address their problem. Of course, there are occasions when some detail is desired by an audience member. There are also occasions when a technical person is in the audience who may care about the details to a much greater extent than the nontechnical audience members. You must try to find a way to pacify the technical person without losing the rest of the audience, such as suggesting a follow-up.

Think of providing technical details like filling a glass. You can always add a bit more to a glass if it isn't full enough, but once the glass overflows you have a big mess. Once the mess is made, you can't take it back. Similarly, you can always add technical details a little bit at a time to work toward what your audience desires. However, once you go too far and lose the audience, it is very hard to get them back. Your strategy should be to always add detail slowly until it is clear you've hit the level that is required and offer no more.

I came across another great analogy for this concept. Only provide a tree trunk to start. If someone wants to understand the branches, then go to that level. If they then ask to understand the leaves, then go to that level. However, if you always drill down to the tiniest details, your presentation will fail with every audience except those wanting the tiniest details. If you always start at a high level and only get more detailed as asked, then you can succeed with every audience you present to!

Years back, a client (I can't recall who) said, "Share the what, so what, and now what. Only go into the how and why if requested." We actually serve ourselves and our sponsors best when we say the least we can to instill confidence that we have the situation handled and that we can provide valuable guidance on what to do with the results we have found. It can be very hard for technical professionals to hold back on the details that we get excited about. It takes discipline to avoid falling into the trap of saying way too much!

Note: Based on my blog *A Common Trap That Undermines Analytics Credibility* (International Institute For Analytics, February 2019).

Tip 17: Focus on How to Use Your Results

When presenting and discussing technical information, it is necessary to interpret requests for clarification or additional detail from the view of the person asking the question. A nontechnical person without your level of understanding will often ask a question using verbiage that, if an expert asked the same thing, could mean something very different than what the nontechnical person is trying to ask.

Imagine going into a car dealership to look at a vehicle and asking how the backup camera system works. If the salesperson (who is a technology fanatic) starts talking about the high-definition OLED screen, the onboard sensors that are scanning the area in real time, and how the trajectory lines are computed and rendered on the screen, you'll probably wish you hadn't asked. Although the salesperson is an expert who is passionate about such details, it is important for the salesperson to determine if the customer is a technology fanatic too before going into such a technical explanation. If you aren't sure what your audience wants, then ask!

When most people ask how the backup camera system works, they really want to know *how to use the backup camera*, not literally how the camera system works. A great response from the salesperson would be, "You'll see what's behind you and a projection of where you are going as you back up. If you hear a beep, then stop!"

Similarly, if a business executive asks, "How do these analytics work?," the desire likely isn't to understand the math, the data issues found, or how the analytics will be deployed on the organization's systems. Rather, the executive likely wants to understand how to use the results. For example, a simple answer might be, "The analytics will provide a probability of response for each customer. You can then decide to make each customer an offer (or not) based on that probability."

The same concept would apply in any technical discipline. If an executive or customer asks during a product presentation, "How does this new glue work?," they probably don't want a lesson on the chemistry behind it. They most likely want to hear, "Although you apply the glue just like you would our other products, this glue will have a bond after drying that is over twice as strong as our standard product."

Always remember when giving a data-driven presentation that when asked, "How does it work?," the real question is almost always, "How do I use it and how will it add value to me?" This is especially true when presenting to a nontechnical audience. Failing to recognize the distinction can lead you to confuse and frustrate the audience. Worse, they may decide you are too technical to be of practical use to them, tune you out, and ignore your findings.

> *Note:* Based on my blog *A Common Trap That Undermines Analytics Credibility* (International Institute For Analytics, February 2019).

Tip 18: Use Analogies to Make an Impact

I suspect this will be one of the more controversial tips in the book. I know many people do not like using analogies and think that it weakens their position. When dealing with other technical people, I can see that argument. If discussing technical issues among technical peers, maybe you should be able to explain things without resorting to an analogy (though I personally still think analogies are helpful even then). However, when dealing with a nontechnical audience, I have found that an analogy can be one of the best ways to help an audience "get" a complex concept.

Two of the most popular analogies I have ever used include one based on fleas trapped in a jar to illustrate innovative thinking and one comparing frozen yogurt shop business models to illustrate why a common analytical architecture needed changing. Both of those probably sound like they would be ridiculous for the purpose I used them, but they really helped people understand how to think differently about a common, complex issue. I typically don't set out to develop an analogy. Instead, as I see people struggling to grasp a given topic, I try different ways to explain it. I often eventually land on an analogy that works and then use it moving forward.

You may notice that in this book there are a lot of places where I illustrate a tip by using an analogy from day-to-day life that doesn't relate to presenting data-driven content. After laying the groundwork with the analogy, I then tie it to presenting data-driven content. My guess is that you probably remember my analogy for some of the tips better than you remember the more technical explanation. If so, that's exactly why you should consider using analogies yourself!

Tip 19: Make Liberal Use of Appendices

This book talks a lot about keeping slides to a minimum and not showing more detail than necessary. However, there are often additional details that you need to make available for later review by your audience. Appendices are where to place any extra information you need to provide. They enable the audience to get the main points quickly as you talk while providing them additional details to review later as desired.

My belief is that appendices are greatly underused and undervalued as a tool to enable a diverse audience to grasp a data-driven presentation, so don't be shy about adding appendices liberally. If appendices are clearly labeled, your audience will easily find the information they want when they review your material later. While you are presenting, you shouldn't display your appendices, of course, but you should alert the audience to the fact that they are present. Figure 19a is a simple slide that lists available appendices. As you tell your story, you can remind the audience when there is an appendix that provides more information on a given topic. Even if the audience doesn't ask to see the appendix as you present, they will be comforted that it is available for later review.

If questions force you to discuss material in one of your appendices, don't default to showing an entire appendix section. Rather, as per Tip 16, show and discuss only the portion of the appendix that enables you to answer the question you were asked before returning to your main presentation. Of course, per Tip 100, never hand out your appendices until after your presentation.

Appendices Available for Review

- Appendix A: Data sources and fields used for the analysis

- Appendix B: Overview of the methodologies utilized

- Appendix C: Relevant articles and papers for further reading

- Appendix D: Project history and charter documents

- Appendix E: Summary of prior efforts to solve this problem

FIGURE 19A A List of Appendices for the Audience

Tip 20: Create a Distinct Leave-Behind Document

Tip 19 focuses on using appendices to include additional information that the audience may want to see. Appendices are but one option. Appendices can be used by themselves or alongside other options, such as those discussed in this tip.

In my field, when there is a very important, high-stakes analysis involving a lot of investment, generating a formal written report to support the live presentation slides can be a necessity. A formal written report is closer to an academic paper in that it will have extensive details on various aspects of the project. Of course, writing this type of report is time-consuming and it only makes sense for high-value initiatives.

A middle option between appendices and a totally separate document is to make use of the "notes" section of PowerPoint so that you can provide additional details to the audience through the printing of the "notes pages" view from the print menu. Using this approach, you can include a good bit more detail than will fit on a slide. At the same time, the format tends to keep your additional comments short so that they fit within one or at most two pages, which won't overwhelm the audience.

I personally like the notes pages approach because it lets me place additional important data and talking points underneath each slide. Then, when I am reviewing my slides before my presentation, I also review the notes. It helps me prepare as well as providing more information to the audience when I provide them the printout. Figure 20a shows an example of how a notes pages printout looks. It is clean and easy to follow. Figure 20b shows how to print the notes pages (Microsoft 365 version).

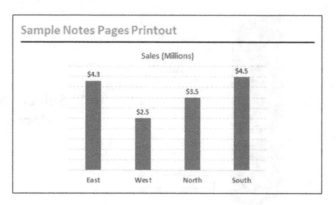

FIGURE 20A Use Notes Pages as a Leave-Behind Document

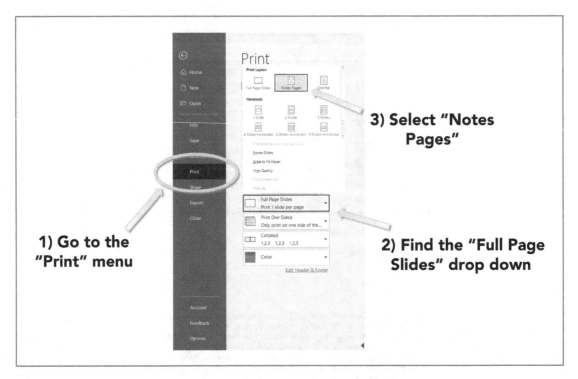

FIGURE 20B How to Print Notes Pages

Tip 21: Create "Launch" Slides

In Tip 23, we talk about using animations to control information flow. Animations are helpful when there are multiple pieces of information you would like to discuss in a set order. Sometimes, however, you will have a topic that is far-reaching but you need flexibility in how you cover it based on audience feedback and reaction. This is where a concept that I call a "launch" slide comes into play.

A launch slide has a high-level summary of a concept. It could be an overview of a framework or a process flow, for example. After explaining the general concept of what is on the launch slide, you might ask the audience what components are of most interest. Then, you launch into a discussion of the topic(s) of most interest. You can even use action settings (see Tip 24) to jump back and forth in an ad hoc fashion to the slides with your drill-down points.

Another option is to leave the launch slide up and just talk to all of the points. A launch slide could stay up for a very long time, so be sure to account for that in your preparations (see Tip 87). By leaving the launch slide up while you dive deeper verbally, you achieve several things:

- You keep the audience fully focused on you and your story.
- You show mastery of the subject matter by being able to talk about any aspect on the fly without slide support. Audiences appreciate when you know your material well enough to go off script!
- Your audience retains the big picture from the launch slide in their minds, which helps keep your drill-down points in the proper larger context.

Figure 21a shows a potential launch slide. In this case, you can discuss the overall product life cycle, each phase at a high level, and also details on each phase without ever leaving this single, illustrative slide. Figure 21b is a classic analytical project flow. You can talk in detail to any or all of the phases without leaving the slide. In both examples, your leave-behind document or appendices can contain the detailed information you discuss.

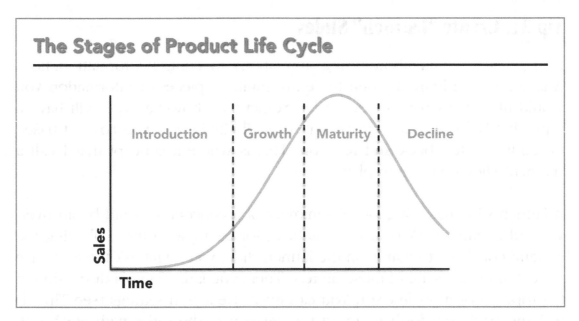

FIGURE 21A A Framework Launch Slide

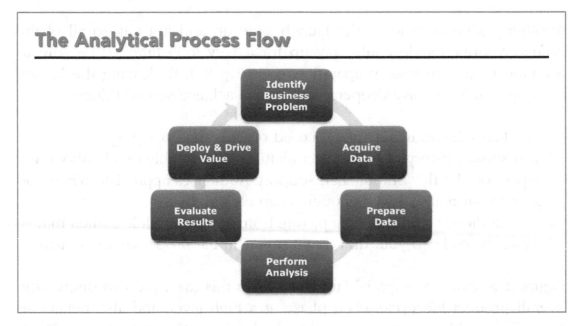

FIGURE 21B A Process Launch Slide

Tip 22: Break Content into Smaller Pieces

It is tempting to provide as much detail as possible on one slide. You can get away with that in an interactive online report or in a detailed leave-behind document because the audience in those settings has as much time as they need to look closely at the content and interpret it. During your live presentation, as we've discussed repeatedly in this book, you want people focused on you and not on analyzing the information on the screen. As a result, you must break your content into smaller, digestible pieces.

Consider a complex dashboard that stakeholders review daily. Because they are used to seeing that dashboard, it is tempting to use the dashboard as a slide during a presentation. However, this will make the slide look over-loaded and will distract the audience. During your presentation, you'll have to talk about one point at a time, so reveal the information one point at a time. Instead of a single slide with lots of information, create multiple slides with targeted, specific pieces of information. Alternatively, use animations as outlined next in Tip 23 to keep the audience focused as your discussion drills down into pieces within a complex slide.

The slide in Figure 22a is simply too busy to be easily digested by an audience (technical or not) while you are speaking. It might be terrific as a leave-behind document, but it will not go over well live. Figure 22b shows one of the charts as a standalone slide that you can talk to. Figure 22c uses an animation method from Tip 23 so each piece is highlighted as you speak to it while the others are deemphasized.

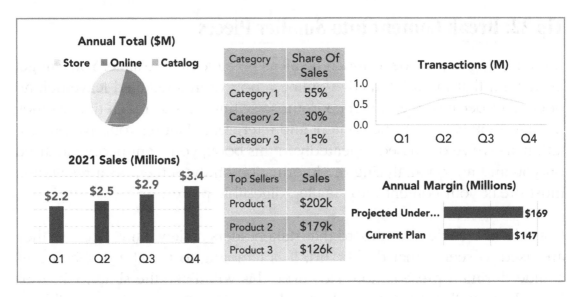

FIGURE 22A Quarterly Dashboard

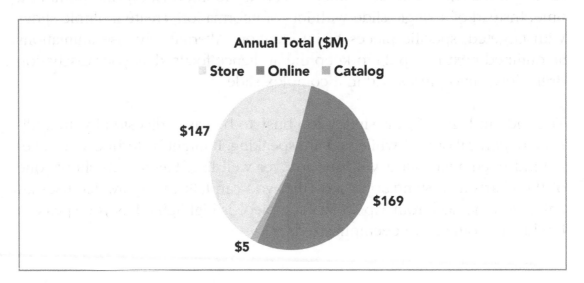

FIGURE 22B Quarterly Dashboard Highlight – Sales by Channel

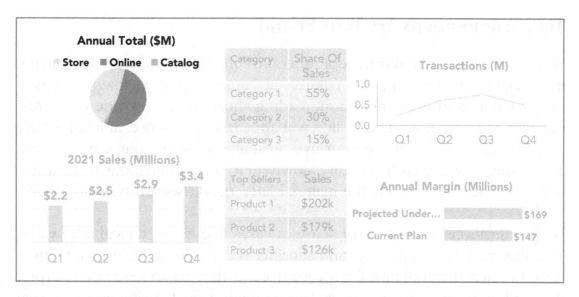

FIGURE 22C Quarterly Dashboard (with Animations)

Tip 23: Animations Are Your Friend

Slide animations are a terrific tool for controlling flow within a slide. Having important information appear one piece at a time keeps the audience focused on your story and stops them from reading ahead. If you provide your presentation as a handout, the full slide will appear. In this sense, animations are another way to differentiate your live presentation from your leave behind. The audience will watch the story slowly unfold via animations in your live talk, but when they review the material later, they'll see everything at once.

Basic animations make a lot of sense in cases like listing critical takeaways. The slide may be a few short and succinct points, but revealing them all at once distracts the audience from your story as they try to read and interpret them all as soon as they appear. Use animation in this situation to reveal each point one at a time as you're ready to discuss it. Similarly, if you have multiple charts on a slide, reveal them one at a time.

Another way to use animations is to highlight items. If compelled to show a large table, highlight what is important by using animations to circle numbers, draw an arrow to them, or enlarge their size. Each method draws the audience's attention where you want it. Figure 23a illustrates these methods (we'll discuss these methods more in Tip 95).

More advanced techniques include not just adding items but removing or changing the look of items. One trick I like to use is to make all but the current item of focus appear mostly transparent. That way, even as I add more to the slide, it is very clear where attention should be. Figure 23b illustrates what this looks like.

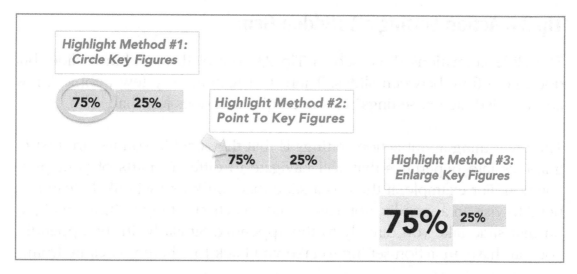

FIGURE 23A Three Animation Options for Highlighting Key Figures

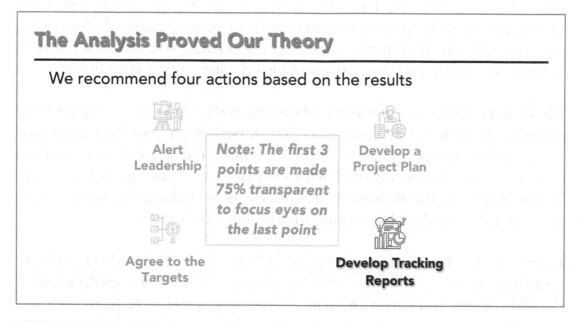

FIGURE 23B Using Transparency Animations

Tip 24: Action Settings: A Hidden Gem

The slide animations discussed in Tip 23 control flow within a slide, but don't help flow between slides. There is a feature very few people know about called "action settings" in PowerPoint that does just that.

The great thing about action settings is that they enable you to turn text or graphics into hyperlinks that will navigate to different parts of your presentation. For example, if there is a slide that you know will likely lead to a need to visit an appendix, you can create an action setting to have an object on that slide take you directly to the appendix. Similarly, in the appendix, you can have an action setting to take you back to where you came from.

This is a powerful tool because it lets you stay in "presentation mode" while being dynamic. You don't need to hit page up or page down repeatedly or exit presentation mode and scroll down to your appendix before going back into presentation mode. Action settings enable you to move between content seamlessly and easily without visibly interrupting your flow.

I have done interactive webinars where the audience votes on which topic out of a few choices they desire me to cover next. Each question on the slide has an action setting to take me to the right place if that question wins. Each topic's content then sends me back to my question slide when I am done. To the audience, the webinar is a seamless flow. Behind the scenes, I am bouncing all over the place within the presentation's slides.

It isn't always clear how many topics I will get through based on audience participation, so I also put an action setting on the logo or copyright text in the slide master and have that go to my wrap-up section. No matter where I am in the presentation, when it is time to end, I can get directly to my wrap-up section with a single click. If you experiment with action settings, I think you'll become a fan very quickly. It will also open the door to new types of presentations, such as the one I described in the prior paragraph.

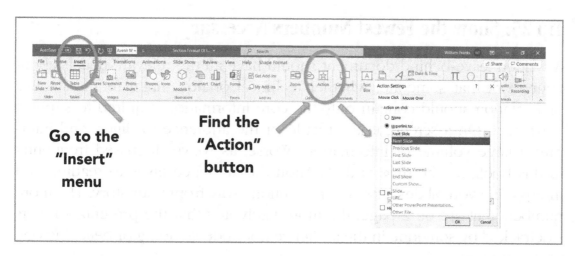

Go to the "Insert" menu

Find the "Action" button

FIGURE 24A How to Apply Action Settings

Figure 24a shows where to find the Action Settings item on the Insert menu in PowerPoint (Microsoft 365 version). The icon is in the middle by default and that's why I think most people miss it. I typically just use the "Hyperlink to:" option in the menu because it usually meets the need. Notice the ability to jump to any specific slide or the slide you last came from, among other options.

Tip 25: Show the Fewest Numbers Necessary

A written leave-behind document should have all the relevant details about your work that someone, whether technical or not, might require. A live presentation should contain only the core information required to support your story. On a screen, it is difficult for the audience to digest and interpret a large volume of information. Worse, as we've discussed frequently in this book, all the time and attention the audience gives to reading and interpreting your slides takes their attention away from your story. The more numbers that are on a page, the more likely it is that the presentation gets sidetracked by someone in the audience not understanding or believing one of the numbers.

Consider a situation in which your company has a standard view of five core products' sales by quarter. It might seem easiest and natural to display the typical five products by four quarters grid of sales that people are used to seeing. The problem with that approach is that you end up with 20 numbers on the slide (not including totals if you also need them). At any point in your presentation, however, you are likely discussing a single specific cell from that table (or just a few related cells). Instead of providing the entire table of data, design each slide to have only the specific data points you plan to discuss at that time.

This approach will keep the audience focused on the important information you're discussing without distracting them with a bunch of other noise. In an extreme case, you might talk about most of the cells in the larger table at some point in your presentation. However, by displaying and discussing just a few numbers at a time, it will make your data-driven presentation more effective and will allow your audience to follow along. The entire 5 × 4 table can be in an appendix, and you can let the audience know that the numbers you're showing are available in the standard grid view they are used to seeing.

Figure 25a shows the full 5 × 4 table while calling out one important fact in the headline. Although it is possible to see what the headline is talking about by looking at the table, it does take effort. You also have to stop yourself

Organic Honey Grew by over 50% This Past Year!

Product	Q1 Sales	Q2 Sales	Q3 Sales	Q4 Sales	Yearly Total Sales
Regular Honey	$4.3M	$4.4M	$4.3M	$4.5M	$17.5M
Premium Honey	$3.1M	$2.9M	$3.0M	$3.1M	$12.1M
Organic Honey	$2.2M	$2.5M	$2.9M	$3.4M	$11M
Peach Honey	$1.1M	$1.0M	$0.9M	$0.9M	$3.9M
Blueberry Honey	$1.0M	$1.1M	$0.9M	$0.8M	$3.8M
Quarter Total	$11.7M	$11.9M	$12.0M	$12.7M	$48.3M

FIGURE 25A Too Much Data Makes It Hard to See the Point

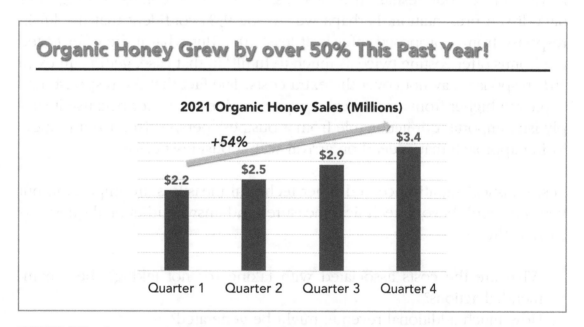

FIGURE 25B Showing Just the Data to Support the Headline

from focusing on all of the other numbers. Figure 25b shows only the numbers that pertain to the headline. This helps the audience focus on what is important to the point you are discussing. In Section 6, we'll discuss more options for clarifying the information you want your audience to take away.

Tip 26: Distinguish Technical Significance from Business Significance

In my field, although statistical significance is commonly assessed, it isn't enough to prove an analysis is a success worthy of action. It is also necessary to determine and communicate how the results are significant from a business and practical perspective. If the audience doesn't find your results to be relevant and actionable, you are just providing noise. The same principle holds true with any other type of technical measure of importance. Who cares if a proposed building can support twice the anticipated maximum stress it will be exposed to if the building is ugly or won't fit in the lot it is targeted for?

Always place your results in a business or practical context during your data-driven presentation. Perhaps we can be 99% confident that the lift in response from a proposed offer is at least 10%. But what if the offer tested is a bonus offer costing twice as much to fulfill? In that case, getting an extra 10% response may not cover the extra costs. The fact that the response rate is proven higher from a statistical perspective doesn't matter because it simply isn't important or actionable from a business perspective. It is a money-losing approach that is dead on arrival with a businessperson.

Yes, statistical significance and other technical measures are important, but you must look beyond technical measures and answer additional questions such as these:

- What are the costs associated with taking (or not taking) the recommended actions?
- How much additional revenue might be generated?
- Is the new approach consistent with the overall corporate strategy?
- Are people available to make the process changes that will be required?
- Are there any regulatory or legal guidelines that need to be accounted for?

Audiences, even if nontechnical, might be comforted to know that something is statistically or technically significant. However, don't expect them to take your presentation and recommendations seriously if you don't clearly point out why the results have business and practical significance as well.

Note: This tip is adapted from my book *Taming the Big Data Tidal Wave* (Wiley, 2012).

Tip 27: Give the Audience Your Headlines

As you design your data-driven presentation, one of the first things you must do is to create an outline that lays out your narrative, the key points that you want to get across to the audience, and the actions you want them to take. You will then build your presentation from that outline. It is a good idea to clue the audience in on the direction you're heading up-front to draw them in from the start (we'll also talk more about this in Tip 28). Let's look at a couple of examples of why this is important.

Virtually all books have some paragraphs on the back cover as well as an introduction section and a table of contents. These all serve to give a potential reader a feel for what the book is about, what it will discuss, and what the reader will get out of the book. Very few people will pick up a book and start reading without having any idea whatsoever what it is about and what type of story it will tell.

For movies or television series, trailers are a ubiquitous method of distilling down key scenes that capture the essence of the flow, style, and tone of a movie or series so that potential viewers can decide if it is for them or not. The trailers don't give away too much, but they do give away enough to get the attention of viewers.

Let's take the same concepts and apply them to your presentation. Do you typically launch into your narrative and assume that the audience will stick with you until the end? That's a mistake. Similar to a book preview or movie trailer, you should explain up-front the general direction you intend to take your presentation. If you understand your audience well (per Tip 5), they will like your introduction and will be willing to give you their attention to hear the whole story. Perhaps some in the audience will realize that your presentation isn't for them. That's okay, too. They can always leave without guilt and they'll be happy you didn't waste their time.

Note that what I am talking about here is more than just an agenda slide. It is the selective revealing, whether verbally, on a slide, or both, of core themes and takeaways that your presentation will provide. Similar to a book cover, you are providing a short overview of your story to get the audience committed. Going through the process of developing your introduction will also force you to think through which of your points are most important and compelling. This, in turn, can lead to changes to the outline you originally designed, creating a positive feedback loop.

Tip 28: Start with Your Recommended Actions

I have seen much debate over the years about whether you should (1) give away your big ideas and recommended actions up-front and then defend them or (2) save the ideas and recommendations for a big reveal after you've woven an exciting narrative and have the audience on the edge of their seat. In an ideal world, saving big ideas until the end would be the way to go. However, our world isn't ideal. Audience members will leave early, they'll get distracted, or you'll field so many questions that you don't have time to do anything but rush through your big ideas in the closing minutes. These real-world realities, among others, will jeopardize the success of your data-driven presentation.

I have come around to the view that the best design approach is to state up-front the big ideas and recommended actions that you plan to substantiate in your presentation. In practice, this will have several benefits. First, everyone will know where you are heading, and if they have a big stake in what you've found they'll be more likely to stay focused if they are made aware that your presentation is leading to something of high relevance to them.

Second, if someone must leave early or if your presentation is derailed by questions, the audience will know what you were working toward. People will be much more likely to give you another meeting to complete your story if they know the ending is compelling. If you are cut off mid-presentation and the audience still doesn't know anything about how it ends, they are likely to just move on. Imagine you are taking your friend to an amazing five-star restaurant as a surprise, and you hit hideous traffic. Not knowing what you have planned, your friend will suggest stopping someplace close to avoid the mess. If you inform your friend of the ultimate five-star destination, however, chances are that they will be willing to sit through a lot more traffic to get there. Similarly, an audience will be willing to allot more time for a follow-up discussion if they know it will be worth their time.

Last, based on the reactions from the audience to your initial reveal, whether positive or negative, you can adjust how much time you spend on various parts of your story to increase focus on those areas that have the most interest (see Tip 102). Sometimes you'll be surprised that points you thought would be a hard sell are well received whereas points you thought would be readily accepted receive substantial resistance.

It is important to note that you will need to actively manage the audience so that they don't start litigating your recommended actions after you reveal them up-front. Make clear that the point of your presentation is to lay out the case for the actions and that you would like the audience to hear you explain and put the ideas in context before debating their merits.

One exception to the rule of starting with your big ideas and recommended actions is if they are highly charged politically or otherwise quite sensitive. In such cases, laying out the end of the story without the buildup and full context can backfire because emotions may run high and be impossible to rein in. It is hard to imagine how starting with, "We need to lay off 40% of our staff" with no context will go over well. It is better to ease an audience into sensitive findings.

Tip 29: Don't Focus on the "What"

Technical people love to discuss details about what they did and, from a technical perspective, why they did it. The harsh reality is that a nontechnical audience doesn't care about the technical aspects of what you did. They care about what you've found, why it matters to them, and what they should do as a result.

Avoid focusing on the *what* aspect of your efforts in terms of what you did and what led you to choose that path technically. Instead focus on the *why* in terms of the practical problem you're solving, the *so what* for the audience, and, most important, the *what now* recommendations. Let's review what each of these is about.

The *why* aspect of your presentation has several components. First, why did you address the problem you're discussing? Second, why is the problem important to the audience? Third, why will the audience benefit from hearing about what you've found?

The *so what* aspect of your presentation ties to why your findings and information matter to the audience. What is the business value of your findings? How will listening to you help the nontechnical audience meet its goals? Help the audience grasp that they have a personal stake in your results.

The *what now* aspect of your presentation entails laying out specific recommendations and actions for the audience to enable them to take full advantage of your findings. Don't make the nontechnical audience connect the dots. Rather, connect those dots for them and give them tangible next steps (see Tip 118).

Figure 29a is mostly about the technical *what*. It isn't very compelling. Figure 29b addresses the *why*, the *so what*, and the *what next*. Doesn't it sound better?

Project Summary

- We built a logistic regression model to predict which customers are most likely to buy our new drink flavor

- We used this model because it is a good fit for binary outcomes of this type

- Based on our tests, the model generates a 25% lift compared to the planned rollout approach

- The model has low false positive and false negative rates

- There are a few data issues that we still need to address

FIGURE 29A An Example of Too Much "What"

We Have a $37M Opportunity with Our New Flavor!

- The last few product rollouts haven't gone as well as expected, in part due to poor customer targeting

- Through our analysis, we found a way to improve first year sales by up to 25% with a few adjustments to the upcoming rollout plan

- Achieving a 25% lift on current projections for our new flavor will generate an extra $37M in the first year

- Our team has generated a list of high potential customers for the marketing team to target

- The processes are built, so with approval we are ready to go!

FIGURE 29B An Example of "Why," "So What," and "What Next"

Developing: Wording and Text

Although any data-driven presentation will require the development of a variety of figures and charts (we'll talk about developing graphics in later sections), the text that you place on your slides and how that text is worded are critically important to audience comprehension. You must get your points across clearly and succinctly while using terms and phrasing that your (often nontechnical) audience can understand. Here are some of the concepts discussed in this section:

- Minimize the number of words on your slides.
- Aggressively avoid technical terms and phrases.
- Ensure everything on your slides can be easily seen by the audience.
- Do not rely on automated spelling and grammar checks.
- Clearly define terms and use those terms consistently.

Perhaps the simplest rule of thumb is to always read the content you develop through the lens of the intended audience. That audience will be largely unfamiliar with the terms and lingo that you and your technical peers use, so make sure you're not displaying text that may as well be a foreign language to them. If the person in your organization who is least knowledgeable about your topic would be able to read and understand your points, then you are on the right path.

Tip 30: Minimize the Number of Words on Your Slides

Tip 3 discussed keeping the audience focused on your story and not your slides, and Tip 6 discussed keeping slides short and to the point. To achieve those goals, you must minimize the number of words on your slides. Although this should be obvious, I have had people defend a slide filled with bullet points simply because they had removed even more additional points. Getting to less words than you started with isn't enough!

This is one tip that I personally continue to struggle with. Typically, when I initially develop a slide, I'll include sentence-length points to get my thoughts down. As I refine the presentation, I focus on shortening my sentences to the core sound bite. It usually takes a couple of passes to get to my final text.

A visual slide shouldn't include the exact words you will say when speaking. That will not look right and will appear long-winded when people read it. At the same time if you speak exactly what is on a slide, you'll sound like a sound-bite machine. How we speak and write is different, so take advantage of that by not worrying about matching the text to your speech.

To reduce your text to a minimum, follow this simple recipe:

- Draft slides initially with no concern for word count. Get your thoughts down per the first pass in Figure 30a.
- Put the presentation aside for a few hours or overnight. Later, make another pass as per the second pass in Figure 30a.
- Iterate until you have shrunk your text down to the essence of what you want to say per the final text in Figure 30a. The goal is getting down to one line, or at most two lines, of a substantively sized font.

- **First Pass – Free Form**
  - The results show that we should do less promotion of Product A in favor of more promotion of Product B due to its increasing popularity

- **Second Pass – Tightened**
  - To improve results, we should promote newly popular Product B more and Product A less

- **Final Text – The Bare Essence**
  - Shift promotional funds from Product A to Product B

FIGURE 30A Evolving Your Points

Tip 31: Use Simple Terms and Definitions

There are common terms and acronyms in any discipline that can be completely unfamiliar and confusing to an audience. Because experts are familiar with such terms, it is easy for them to put terms in a data-driven presentation without carefully defining them. The speaker understands the concept but can't neglect to provide a simple definition that the audience will grasp.

In my field of analytics, terms tied to response model evaluation include *precision, recall, sensitivity, specificity,* and more. Even being in the field, I often must think for a minute to remember which of these opaque terms means what. I prefer to use the plain English descriptions instead.

Sensitivity is the true positive rate and *specificity* is the true negative rate of a model's predictions. Why anyone would prefer to discuss *sensitivity* instead of *true positive rate* is beyond me. I like this example because *specificity* and *sensitivity* are two terms I always get mixed up because they sound similar and are tied to similar concepts. As an audience member, would you rather see Figure 31a or Figure 31b? People are far more likely to understand and remember an explanation of *true negative rate* than *specificity*. Whatever your field, you can find analogous examples.

Accuracy	90%
Sensitivity	92%
Specificity	86%

FIGURE 31A Model Performance – Technical Version

Percent Correctly Classified	90%
True Positive Rate	92%
True Negative Rate	86%

FIGURE 31B Model Performance – Layperson's Version

As you develop your content, make sure that you can explain all terms to your audience. In the prior example, although most audience members would easily understand the concept of a true positive rate, they'll have a hard time remembering the term *sensitivity* even if you define it. It makes it easier on you and the audience to use the simpler terminology. Also monitor the audience to identify when further definition is warranted based on confused looks in the room.

Tip 32: Don't Use Technical Terms

Tip 31 talks about simple terms and definitions. A further extension is that one way to quickly turn off a nontechnical audience is to use technical terms that they don't understand, especially given that they usually start with an assumption that you might be too technical for them. That assumption may not be fair, but it is reality that the assumption is often made. If you play into that assumption, you risk losing the audience and having them not listen to your story.

Few people purposely include terms their audience won't understand. The problem is that there are terms technical people use so often that they just seem standard to them. It is easy to forget that your audience may not hear the same terms you do every day. I can't tell you how many times in my consulting work that a client started throwing out internal corporate terms to the point I had no idea what they were saying. The clients were never trying to lose me. They just didn't think about the fact that I didn't use those terms every day like they did.

I get annoyed when someone who is technical in a different field than mine starts throwing around terms I don't understand. I'll bet you do, too. There are even rare people who like to throw out technical terms to show how smart they are. Don't be that person!

It takes a concerted effort to prevent yourself from using technical terms. As you develop your presentation, force yourself to review it and identify places where you need to either add explanation or change terms. You'll never hear me utter *monotonicity* or *heteroscedasticity* in a business presentation even though those are actually meaningful statistical terms!

Tip 33: Clarify Your Definitions

While using simple terms and avoiding technical ones, it is important to consistently clarify the definition of the terms you do use in your data-driven presentation. Whether shown on the screen or expressed verbally, the audience needs to know how a term has been defined when you use it.

If you're using a common term, provide a quick refresher for the audience. Before showing a median value, for example, first say, "Recall that the median is the point at which 50% of the readings are higher and 50% of the readings are lower." Audience members who already know this won't mind your validation, but those who didn't recall this will be grateful that they now understand what you are saying. If you are introducing a new metric the audience may not be familiar with, add a slide just on that metric's definition and use and spend sufficient time explaining it.

It is also important to ensure that your audience is clear on which definition you are using when there are multiple options. Figure 33a shows a compelling argument about increased margin. However, which margin is it? The margin as reported to Wall Street? Gross margin? Margin as computed by the product team? There are often multiple definitions for terms such as *margin* within a large company. If you don't make clear which definition you are using, then people may interpret it differently. That will lead to confusion and misunderstandings.

Figure 33b clearly states which margin is being shown. There might still be lively debate about whether this definition for margin is the right one for the situation, but at least the audience knows what they're seeing. Leaving definitions unclear will lead to misunderstandings and needless debate during your presentation.

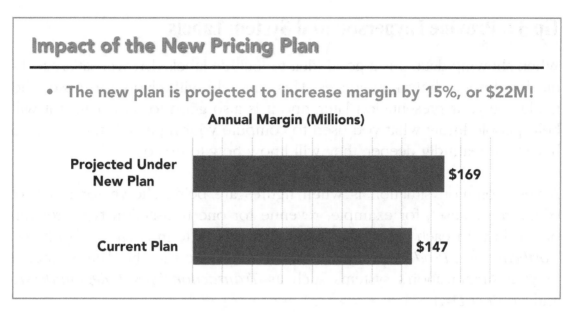

FIGURE 33A Slide with an Unclear Metric Definition

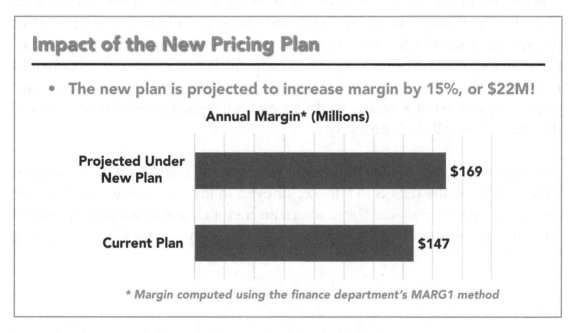

FIGURE 33B Same Slide with the Metric Defined Clearly

Tip 34: Provide Layperson and System Labels

When showing data, it is a good idea to include labels that will satisfy technical and nontechnical audiences. This will help with clarity for those who might see your presentation later, and it is also good to do because it will help people know what you used to compute your figures. If they want to have their team dig deeper, they will know how to do so.

A very common situation is when figures are being shown for a subset of a large dataset, for example, revenue for one transaction type, region, or product. In each case, there is the layperson's term such as *Purchases, Northeast,* and *Product A.* There is also the specific way the data is labeled in your organization's systems such as *TransactionType=P, RegionId=NE,* and *ProductID=A.*

It is helpful to provide the system labels along with the layperson's terms as illustrated in Figure 34a. By showing the exact way the data is identified in the system from which it was retrieved, you provide transparency and make it easier for others to build on your work. Audience members who would never run a query will just ignore the system labels, but for those who want to run a query (or ask others to do so on their behalf), the provided labels ensure that they'll do it properly.

Although Figure 34a shows the system labels in the chart itself, it is also possible to include the details in a footer or even in the notes pages so that they are part of your handout. These alternate methods are especially appropriate when the system label is more complex than in Figure 34a.

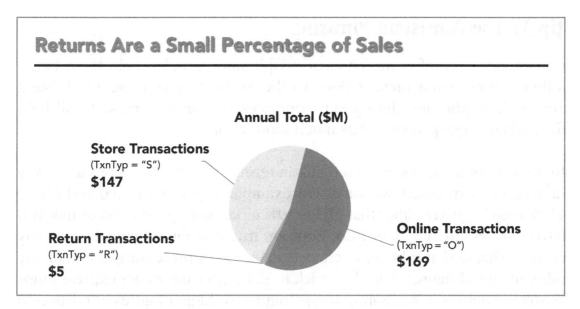

FIGURE 34A Chart Including System Labels

Tip 35: Use Consistent Phrasing

Consistency is comforting for most people and can also help them better follow a data-driven presentation. To the extent that you use a consistent approach to phrasing throughout your presentation materials, it will help the audience grasp your points much more easily.

In my field of analytics, we often talk in terms of probabilities or ratios. Any ratio can be expressed two ways. For example, if you have $100 and I have $150, then I can say either that I have 50% more money than you or that you have 33% less money than I do. Both are true and either is mathematically correct. That said, it is better to choose a method of presenting ratios (or any other technical figures) and then stick to it. In this case, either express ratios as smaller figures in relation to bigger figures or bigger figures in relation to smaller figures.

Figure 35a has bullets that switch between a focus on response and a focus on nonresponse. That makes it hard to follow. Because response is a good thing, Figure 35b focuses on response. By sticking to one approach, Figure 35b is easier to digest and comparing the points directly is possible. Although two of the statements discuss lowering our chance of response, it is far easier to compare an increase in response probability to a decrease in response probability than it is to compare an increase in response probability to an increase in nonresponse probability, as is required by Figure 35a.

- Spending of $10k or more = a 10% increase in **response**

- Spending of $100 or less = a 20% increase in **non-response**

- Premium membership = a 30% increase in **response**

- Recent complaints = a 15% increase in **non-response**

FIGURE 35A Inconsistent and Confusing Phrasing

- Spending of $10k or more = a 10% increase in **response**

- Spending of $100 or less = a 30% decrease in **response**

- Premium membership = a 30% increase in **response**

- Recent complaints = a 10% decrease in **response**

FIGURE 35B Consistent Phrasing

Tip 36: If It Can't Be Read, Don't Display It

Documents often have publication references, image source credits, hyperlinks for more information, and so on. These are usually included using small text so as not to distract from the main point of a page. This is fine in a written document. When presenting to a live audience, it looks sloppy and it will annoy the audience if they can't see what's on the slide.

A simple rule is that if something will not be readable to the live audience when projected on the screen, then do not display it. Just because it is supporting material doesn't mean you should violate Tip 37 by shrinking your text too much. If information isn't important enough to make it big enough for everyone to read during the live presentation, it isn't needed on the slide.

The solution is simple. Just delete small supporting text from your slides for your live presentation while keeping it in the handout version and/or notes. This way, the audience will have all the information they need, but at the time they need it. Figures 36a and 36b show the same slide with and without the supporting items, respectively. Figure 36b looks cleaner and everything on it is readable. You don't want people going to additional reading material during your presentation anyway, so don't offer the option!

One exception to this rule is the copyright notice often placed at the bottom of a slide. In case someone takes a picture or screenshot, it is worth including the small copyright notice. Even though it won't be readable, people know what it is, and if they receive a slide capture from someone, they'll be aware that it is copyrighted.

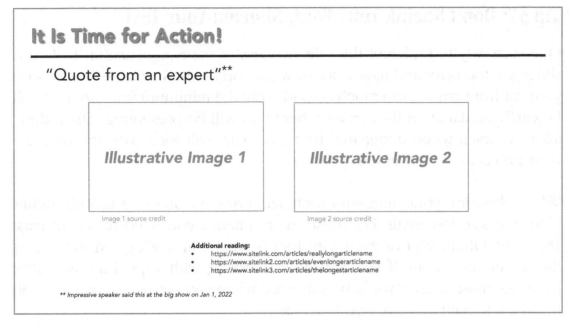

FIGURE 36A Chart with Hard-to-Read Text

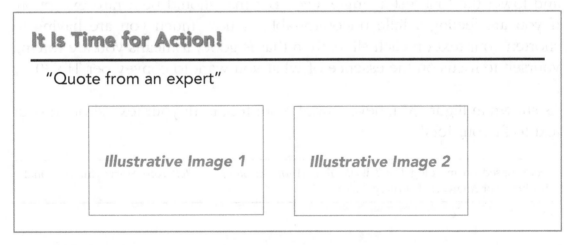

FIGURE 36B Same Chart without Hard-to-Read Text

Tip 37: Don't Shrink Your Font, Shorten Your Text

One sure way to undercut the effectiveness of your presentation is if your slides are too busy and have a lot of words on them. A reliable way to stop yourself from writing too much is to identify the minimum font size that will be easily readable on the screen where you will be presenting. Then, don't allow yourself to go under that font size. This will force you to compress your points as we discussed in Tip 30.

When choosing your minimum font size, error on one size too big rather than one size too small. For most environments, you need to use at least 18pt font. Often, 20pt or even 24pt font is what will work given the size of the screen and room. If you're used to working with 12pt, 14pt, and 16pt fonts like most people, you'll be surprised when you see how much less will fit on a line with an increased font size.

In a case where only one word is slipping to a second line, you might cheat and lower the font just a single level. But that should be a rare exception. If you are feeling a little uncomfortable at how much you are having to shorten your text on each slide, then that is good. It means you are forcing yourself to focus on the essence of what you want to convey per Tip 30.

As shown in Figure 37a, never shrink your font to fit your text, shorten your text to fit your font!

> *Note:* Based on my blog *Don't Write Your Analytics Story . . . Tell Your Story!* (International Institute For Analytics, February 2020).

- **Original Text – Much Too Long!**
  - If You Have To Shrink Your Font Size To Fit Your Text Because It Is Running Over, Then Your Font Isn't Too Big … Your Text Is Too Long!!!

- **Shrink The Font To Fit – Not Readable!**
  - If You Have To Shrink Your Font Size To Fit Your Text Because It Is Running Over, Then Your Font Isn't Too Big … Your Text Is Too Long!!!

- **Shorten The Text – Much Better!**
  - If You Can't Fit Your Text, It Is Too Long

FIGURE 37A Never Shrink Your Font, Shorten Your Text

Tip 38: Use Appropriate Spacing

No matter the size of your text, you need to make it easy to read. Tip 37 dealt with how long a text point is. This tip deals with how points are spaced from each other. Make sure you include appropriate spacing between lines, paragraphs, and bullet points. As you can see in Figure 38a, having tight spacing makes the slide hard to read and looks awful. Always check the spacing in any template you are using as some come with small spacing as the default.

Although Figure 38b is much easier to read, the only difference is that the spacing between the bullets has been increased. Luckily, it is very easy to adjust spacing. In PowerPoint, simply highlight your text, right click, and pick the item "Paragraph . . . ." Always choose line spacing no tighter than "single." I also always add extra space before or after bullets to add additional separation. My preference is spacing before or after each line that is about one half to two thirds of your font size. So, if you're using a 24pt font, use additional spacing of 12pt to 18pt.

Borrowing from Tip 37, if you ever find yourself shrinking your spacing because you have too many bullets to fit on the slide, it is better to lose some bullets or to create an additional slide than to shrink the spacing. Also note that although the spacing rule applies to paragraphs as well as bullets, you won't be having paragraphs on a slide for a live presentation, will you? I hope not!

> - I do not know why some people compress text spacing
> - People sometimes even use less than single spacing
> - They combine that with no extra padding before or after points
> - It doesn't look nice and is hard to read
> - It is easy to avoid this problem

FIGURE 38A Spacing That Is Too Tight

- I do not know why some people compress text spacing

- People sometimes even use less than single spacing

- They combine that with no extra padding before or after points

- It doesn't look nice and is hard to read

- It is easy to avoid this problem

FIGURE 38B Appropriate Spacing

Tip 39: Use the Same Font throughout Your Presentation

People like consistency, including in a data-driven presentation. Presentations that have a wide range of fonts, especially on a single page, are distracting and hard to read. Ideally, you will pick a single font and use it throughout your presentation. The consistent look and feel will enable the audience to focus on your content rather than noticing another font. Although you want to keep the text on your slides to a minimum, even that minimal text will benefit from consistency.

What specific font you use is not as important as using a fairly standard one. Do not choose an extreme font such as **ALGERIAN**, Curlz MT, or **snap ITC** in a business setting. They are simply too jarring, unusual, and hard to read. Stick with easy-to-read fonts like Arial, Calibri, or Verdana. Notice that different fonts take up different amounts of space. All of the fonts in this paragraph are the same font size, yet they appear to vary quite a bit in size nonetheless.

It is okay to use two or three fonts if you use each in specific places, for example, one font for headers, one font for your primary text, and another font for labels, footers, and other miscellaneous items. A different font for headers, for instance, can help to further differentiate the header from the other information. You can also consider using **bold**, *italics*, or ***both*** to differentiate different areas of text even while using the same font.

Figure 39a looks inconsistent and hard to read because of the different fonts used. It is intentionally extreme to illustrate the point.

Although Figure 39b uses only two fonts, the fact that the fonts switch in the middle of the bullet points makes the slide look sloppy. I see people make this error quite a bit and it is often caused by cutting and pasting text from different sources and not noticing that the fonts are different in each source.

- Using a variety of fonts on a slide is distracting
- **It also looks sloppy**
- People often paste text and don't realize the font changed
- It is hard to think of cases where the use of a variety of fonts make sense
- **Flashy fonts may get attention, but you want the attention on you!**

FIGURE 39A Multiple Fonts Don't Look Right

- Using a variety of fonts on a slide is distracting
- It also looks sloppy
- **People often paste text and don't realize the font changed**
- It is hard to think of cases where the use of a variety of fonts make sense
- Flashy fonts may get attention, but you want the attention on you!

FIGURE 39B Cutting and Pasting Can Lead to Different Fonts

Always be careful to check your fonts after pasting from another source and make it a practice to paste raw text without formatting to ensure you do not override the presentation default.

Figure 39c uses a consistent font throughout. This looks cleaner and more appealing.

- Using a variety of fonts on a slide is distracting
- It also looks sloppy
- People often paste text and don't realize the font changed
- It is hard to think of cases where the use of a variety of fonts make sense
- Flashy fonts may get attention, but you want the attention on you!

FIGURE 39C A Single, Consistent Font Looks Best

Tip 40: Beware the Missing Font

If you build and present a data-driven presentation using your own computer, missing fonts will never be a problem because you obviously can't build a presentation with your computer using a font that isn't on your computer. Most companies will install the same fonts on everyone's computer. So, you are almost always fine when sharing within your organization, too. But using a computer from outside your organization won't always work out well.

If you copy a PowerPoint file to a different computer, and if that computer doesn't have your font, PowerPoint will substitute a default font for yours. Although that sounds great, you must remember that different fonts take different amounts of space (see Tip 39). If the replacement font is sized differently, you can end up with headers and text points wrapping to a new line in places that they did not originally. This will make the slides look sloppy with headers bleeding into the main slide area and text becoming hidden behind graphics, among other issues.

Always check that your PowerPoint looks okay on a different computer as soon as you copy it over. If your font was replaced and your slides now look funky, you have a few options.

- Change the font on the new computer to something similar in size to yours so that everything still fits properly.
- Shrink the size of the text in affected spots just slightly (very slightly per Tip 37!) so that it once again fits. Usually, only a single word will wrap, so a slight decrease in font size fixes the issue.
- Expand the size of the affected text containers so they are wider than the text.
- Present from a PDF instead of the PPT. Although you'll lose any animations, a PDF doesn't depend on local font availability because a PDF embeds the fonts within the document.
- Use your own computer after all, though in some settings this isn't possible.

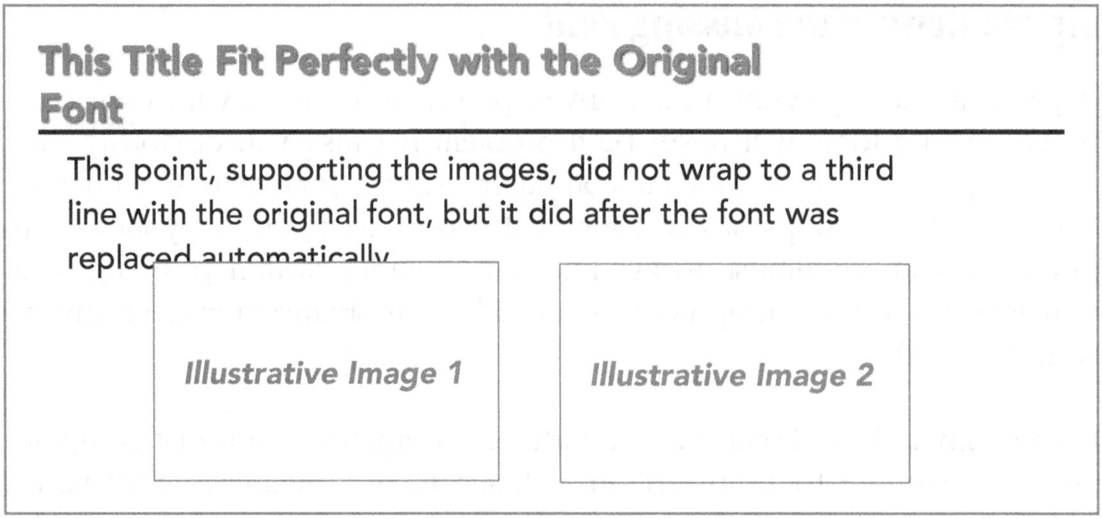

This Title Fit Perfectly with the Original Font

This point, supporting the images, did not wrap to a third line with the original font, but it did after the font was replaced automatically

Illustrative Image 1   *Illustrative Image 2*

FIGURE 40A Impact of a Missing Font

Most of the occasions when I have seen the missing font problem arise (including the first time it happened to me!), the speaker didn't see the problem until after their presentation began. At that point, it is too late to do anything but apologize and grimace each time a slide looks bad. Figure 40a illustrates how a missing font can ruin the look of a slide. None of the text wrapped with the original font.

Tip 41: Address Every Agenda Item Listed

Although this is an obvious mistake to avoid, I have seen many people show an agenda at the start of their presentation and then never discuss one or more items listed on the agenda. For people paying attention, it will not only confuse them and make them wonder if they missed something, but it will lower your credibility and make your data-driven presentation appear incomplete and/or disorganized.

The way this issue typically arises is that multiple drafts of the presentation are generated before the final version is blessed. Often, the agenda slide is one of the first developed, and once you've looked at any slide too many times, it is hard to see it with fresh eyes and realize that something needs to change. If an item was initially on your agenda, but then you decided to cut it out, it is very easy to forget to go back and adjust the agenda slide.

In Figure 41a, the agenda includes an item comparing today's results to those of another recent project. Perhaps it was decided that the comparison was too politically charged or that there wasn't enough time and so the section was removed. The item is still in the agenda and must be removed from it.

A corollary to this tip is to make sure your agenda items are still in the right order in case you reordered topics. The way to avoid these mistakes is to always double-check your agenda slides after your presentation is complete.

You also need to keep the audience appraised of your progress through the agenda, which we'll discuss next in Tip 42.

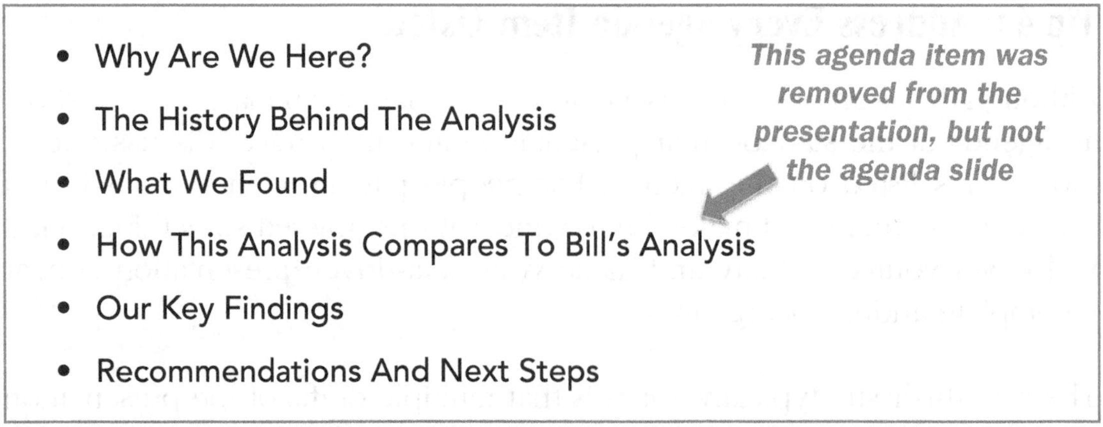

- Why Are We Here?

- The History Behind The Analysis

- What We Found

- How This Analysis Compares To Bill's Analysis

- Our Key Findings

- Recommendations And Next Steps

This agenda item was removed from the presentation, but not the agenda slide

FIGURE 41A Today's Agenda

Tip 42: Identify When an Agenda Item Is Covered

As you cover every agenda item listed, per Tip 41, you must also make it clear to your audience that you have done so. You don't want the audience to have to keep a tally in their head of what's been covered. You also don't want them to look at the handout later and have to work to determine where each agenda item is covered.

The simple way to ensure that the audience knows you are covering an agenda item is to explicitly label the content tied to that agenda item. If you have only one or two slides for a given agenda item, then use the header to call out the agenda item being covered as in Figure 42a. If you have a lot of slides for a given agenda item, then use a section break slide as in Figure 42b.

Unless you have a very short presentation with only a slide or two per agenda item, the section break approach works better. It makes it very clear what each section covers when presenting live and in the printed version. Section breaks also free up valuable header space to be used for something other than identifying the agenda item covered.

Although using section breaks will add to your slide count, you'll learn in Tip 87 that you should focus on time and not slide count. In a live presentation, you'll move past the section headers very quickly while also getting the audience ready for what is coming next. The time impact is negligible and so the extra slide is worthwhile.

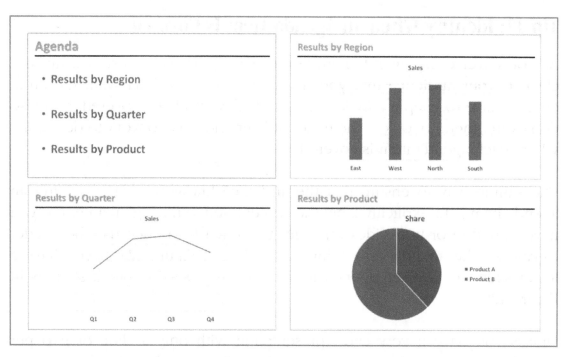

FIGURE 42A Use an Agenda Slide with Headers for Short Sections

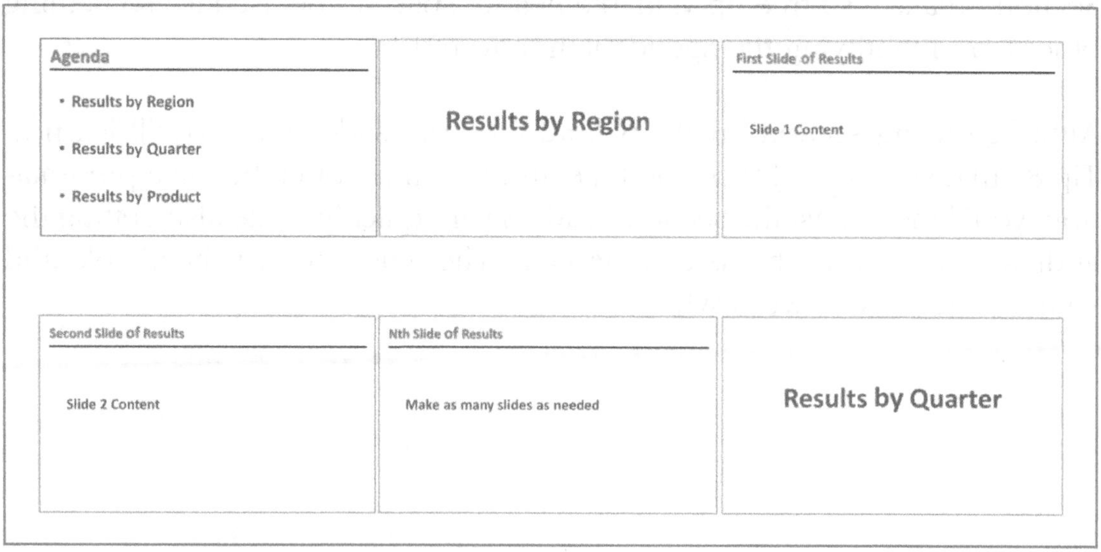

FIGURE 42B Use Section Breaks for Longer Sections

Tip 43: Spellcheck Is Not Always Your Friend

Avoiding misspelled words and bad grammar likely aren't things that you need to be convinced to do. I don't think anyone would argue the fact that spelling and grammar errors detract from your credibility when you display them on a screen. However, I see misspelled words and incorrect verb tenses all the time in presentations.

One reason for these errors is that many people mistakenly rely primarily on automated spelling and grammar checking functions. Although today's automated tools are good, they are not foolproof. Worse, if you rely on them as your primary proofreader, then you'll get lazier and lazier over time when it comes to policing yourself.

Although it is tedious, I always make myself set aside anything I've written for at least a few hours before I come back to it. When I look at it with fresh eyes, I not only clean up and shorten what I've written (per Tip 30) but I also focus on spelling and grammar. What I have found is that even in a relatively short blog, I must override the spelling and grammar check recommendations at least once or twice. This works out to at least one spelling and grammar override for every several hundred words. That's a lot! Figure 43a shows some examples where a built-in spelling and grammar check will lead you astray if you accept its advice.

Note also that when discussing technical content, you often use words that are common within the discipline being discussed but which will not be common enough to be in the spellchecker's dictionary. You'll be on your own to make sure such words are spelled correctly (but use them sparingly per Tip 32).

- **The data is bad. The data are bad.**
  - *There is much debate about if "data" is plural or singular. Spellcheck will accept each, so you can be wrong either way!*

- **It doesn't matter what Bill say about it.**
  - *Grammar check does not catch that "say" should be "says"*

- **We need some MAJIC to fix this**
  - Words in caps will not be spell checked by default

FIGURE 43A Incorrect Spelling and Grammar Check Results

Tip 44: Charts and Images Are Misspelling Factories

When dealing with charts, graphs, and images, you must be especially careful! Spelling and grammar checking software will not scan such content for you and so any errors you make will be carried right through to the audience if you don't find them yourself through manual inspection.

I have had more than one occasion when I created a chart, missed a typo, and then included that chart in a presentation before I (or worse, an audience member) caught the error. Beyond your usual diligence with text content, your charts, graphs, and images require even more attention and diligence. You must check *every single word* in such content personally if you want to avoid embarrassing errors.

Figure 44a is intentionally extreme in the number of typos it contains, yet not one of the obvious typos was flagged by the spelling and grammar checker!

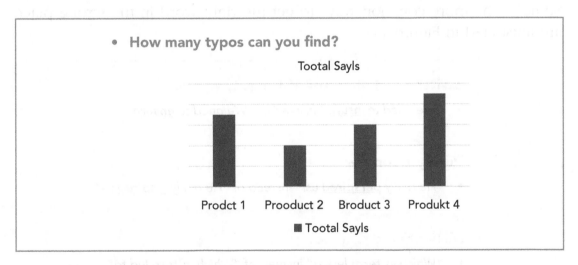

FIGURE 44A Graphs Are Not Checked for Spelling or Grammar!

Tip 45: Beware the Right Word, Wrong Place

An easy mistake to make, and one that is devilishly hard to find, is to use a word that is correctly spelled but use it in the wrong place. These errors are particularly hard to find for two reasons. First, spelling and grammar checkers will think everything looks fine. Second, as you read what you've written, your mind will tend to see what you *meant to say* rather than what you *actually did say*. Even a proofreader can miss this type of error as the proofreader's brain substitutes the logically intended word for the one present.

There is no way to find word substitution errors outside of a careful proofreading of everything in your presentation. One trick someone once taught me is to review content backwards (from bottom to top and right to left) to find errors like this. When reading the content in reverse, it does not flow in a logical fashion and your brain is better able to look at each word and phrase as a standalone entity.

Some of the more common ways to get the right word in the wrong place are illustrated in Figure 45a.

- **Switching similar, but different, words**
  - *"We need to **insure**" instead of "We need to **ensure**"*

- **Purely wrong word**
  - *"He really **perspired** us!" instead of "He really **inspired** us"*

- **Misstating a common phrase**
  - *"Which in **term** led to" instead of "Which in **turn** led to"*

FIGURE 45A Beware the Right Word, Wrong Place

Tip 46: Keep Your Text Horizontal

We almost always read text that is written horizontally. In fact, it is very rare in our daily lives to see text that is anything but horizontal. As a result, our brains have difficulty reading text that is either slanted or pivoted. One place where we do sometimes come across text that flows in different directions is in charts and graphs.

It is not uncommon to have the text on a vertical axis of a chart pivoted 90 degrees so that it reads from top to bottom. Or to have the text pivoted at a 45-degree angle to fit more words in the available space. To make it easy for your audience to interpret, however, avoid using anything but horizontal text whenever possible. This means avoiding charts and graphs that have no option to leave text horizontal.

Figure 46a shows a typical graph displayed in two suboptimal ways: first, with slanted labels below the bars; second, with rotated text so it reads vertically. Both versions are harder to read than Figure 46b, which simply pivots the graph to horizontal so that the labels can be written horizontally too.

The less load you put on your audience's brain, the better they'll be able keep their focus on you and your story. I would be surprised if any readers don't find the chart in Figure 46b to be far easier to consume than either of the charts in Figure 46a.

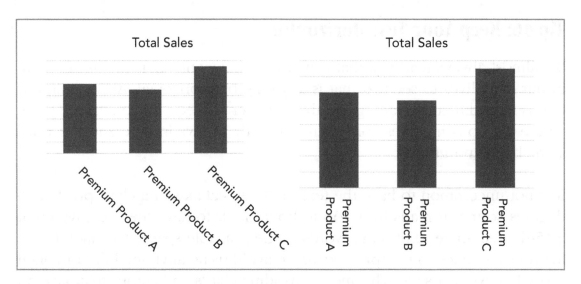

FIGURE 46A Non-Horizontal Text Is Hard to Read

FIGURE 46B Horizontal Text Is Much Easier to Read

Developing: Numbers and Labels

For any data-driven presentation, numbers will be front and center. You'll have numbers explaining the work you did, numbers summarizing what you found, and numbers quantifying the potential impact of those findings. This section will discuss how to make those numbers audience friendly. Here are some of the concepts discussed in this section:

- Use the proper level of precision.
- Format numbers to match the context.
- Clearly label all numbers shown.
- Explicitly label the scale of charts.
- Check that your numbers actually make sense.

With the simple tricks found in this section, you will enable the numbers that you show to convey the message you need to convey while minimizing the effort required for your audience to consume and interpret the information. Your goal is to communicate to your audience the larger trends, patterns, and outcomes your work uncovered while using the fewest numbers possible.

How you label and format your numbers will have a big impact on how your presentation looks and how it is comprehended. Of course, the better your presentation looks and the more it is comprehended by the audience, the more likely it will be successful!

Tip 47: Use Consistent Precision

When you show numbers, you want to make it as easy for your audience to digest the numbers as possible. One way to do this is to ensure that your tables have a consistent format across rows and columns. Having a mix of formats for the same type of data makes it harder for the audience to read.

Note that what format you choose isn't as important as picking a format and sticking with it. Should you show one decimal place or two? Error on as few as necessary, but if it is a toss-up, just pick a format and then use it consistently.

In Figure 47a, you can see that there are different formats for the weights of different melons. This is distracting. In Figure 47b, all weights are rounded to the nearest tenth of a pound. The consistency makes it easier to read the information and to compare across melons.

Melon Farm Productivity

Farm	Average Watermelon Weight (lbs)	Average Honeydew Weight (lbs)	Average Cantaloupe Weight (lbs)
Bill's Farm	20	5.326	3.95
Joe's Farm	21	6.593	4.47
Sue's Farm	22	5.718	5.13
Pat's Farm	20	5.935	4.86

FIGURE 47A Inconsistent Precision Does Not Look Good

Melon Farm Productivity

Farm	Average Watermelon Weight (lbs)	Average Honeydew Weight (lbs)	Average Cantaloupe Weight (lbs)
Bill's Farm	20.4	5.3	4.0
Joe's Farm	21.2	6.6	4.5
Sue's Farm	22.9	5.7	4.7
Pat's Farm	20.7	5.9	4.1

FIGURE 47B Consistent Precision Looks Better

The same concept applies across all types of numbers. Either show dollars and cents or just dollars. Either show dates as MM/DD/YYYY or as YYYY-MM-DD. Either center, right, or left justify the numbers in a table. In all cases, be consistent.

Sometimes it does make sense to have one column of numbers show more decimal places than another if the columns represent very different measures that require different levels of precision (see Tip 49). For example, a person's height can be shown to the nearest inch but the size of their teeth might make sense to show to a tenth of an inch. In such a situation, make sure each column is consistent within itself.

Tip 48: Use Only the Precision Required to Make Your Point

People love to be precise with numbers, and that is not usually a bad thing. However, do not let your love of exactness detract from the point you are trying to make in a data-driven presentation. There are occasions when you have data that needs to be accurate to a very precise level. That does not always mean that you should present that level of detail. Often, too much precision is distracting and not needed.

For example, it is not uncommon to see a comparison of sales for two products. If you put a comparison slide together, you might have exact figures approved by the finance team down to the penny. However, most of the time, showing data at that level will make your chart harder to interpret and will make it more difficult for the audience to see your point.

Figure 48a shows sales data down to the penny and percentages to the thousandths. It makes the table wider and requires the audience to compare complex numbers. The main point is that Yummy Flavor has approximately five times the sales of Yucky Flavor. It does not require sales to the penny to make that point, nor does it require percentages to the thousandths.

Yummy Flavor Outsold Yucky Flavor 5 to 1!

Product	2021 Sales	Percent of 2021 Sales
Yummy Flavor	$509,274,185.45	83.438%
Yucky Flavor	$101,090,925.81	16.562%

FIGURE 48A Too Much Precision Is a Distraction

Yummy Flavor Outsold Yucky Flavor 5 to 1!

Product	2021 Sales	Percent of 2021 Sales
Yummy Flavor	$509M	83%
Yucky Flavor	$101M	17%

FIGURE 48B Less Precision Is Often More Effective

Figure 48b has been expressed in millions of dollars and full percentage points. The table is smaller, and the numbers take less mental energy to absorb and compare. The point is made clearly and succinctly. By expressing the figures in millions, it has made the numbers shorter and easier to interpret while also accurately reflecting the precision level required to make the point.

A great rule of thumb is to show the level of precision where a difference would lead to a change in decision.

Tip 49: Match Precision to Accuracy Level

There is a level of accuracy that can be expected from whatever instrument makes a measurement. For example, a measuring tape read by your eyes might be accurate within ¼ inch, whereas a laser-based measurement might be accurate to 1/1,000[th] of an inch. Your audience will assume that if you are showing a number to three decimal places, then the measurement is precise enough to be accurate to that level. So, make sure that it is.

Precision level can be especially problematic if you are making predictions using statistical or machine learning models. The various parameters in a model will all have margins of error, as will the final prediction. When predicting the percentage lift for an upcoming promotion, even a good model might only be accurate to within a few percentage points. It is inconceivable that a model would be accurate to 1/10 of a percent. The first example in Figure 49a shows a percentage that is certainly displayed to more decimal places than appropriate.

To ensure the audience interprets your numbers in the correct context, round them to the level that matches your accuracy level. Standard software tools will output numbers with many decimal places by default, so be sure not to just use them as is. The second example in Figure 49a has rounded the prediction to a more realistic level.

Consider showing a range when the uncertainty level is quite high and accuracy quite low. This will help the audience interpret the data properly by forcing them to realize that the best you can do is provide a broad range. The last example in Figure 49a makes the presence of uncertainty very clear.

Remember also (per Tip 26) to account for technical and business significance.

- **Rarely is data accurate to extremely precise levels**
  - *Predicted Response Rate:* **10.2453%**

- **Data is often only roughly accurate**
  - *Predicted Response Rate:* **10%**

- **When confidence is very low, consider showing a range**
  - *Predicted Response Rate:* **9.8% - 10.6%**

FIGURE 49A Match Precision to Confidence Level

Tip 50: Always Format Numbers

Whenever you show numbers, always format them, for example, by using comma separators to help the audience digest large numbers. In other words, never show 7532523 or $2720659 but instead show 7,532,523 or $2,720,659. It is almost impossible for an audience to read and interpret numbers bigger than four digits without the comma separators. In addition, the separators enable the audience to quickly gauge the magnitude of the numbers (millions, billions, and so on) so that they can make order of magnitude comparisons.

Many technical software packages will output raw numbers by default, so when you direct output into a table or graph, you'll need to apply an appropriate format to the numbers yourself. Although it is simple to apply the format, it is very easy to cut and paste the software's output and forget to do the formatting. You certainly don't like when someone shows you large numbers with no commas, so don't show such numbers to your audience!

Figure 50a is a simple graph showing numbers without the commas so that it is very hard to read. Figure 50b is the same graph, but it much easier to read with the commas present. However, it violates Tip 48 by showing too much detail. Unless there is the unusual need to show exact results, Figure 50c is even better because it enables the numbers to be more easily interpreted and compared.

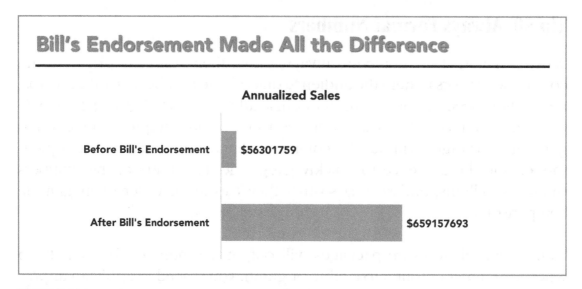

FIGURE 50A Without Formatting, Numbers Can't Be Read

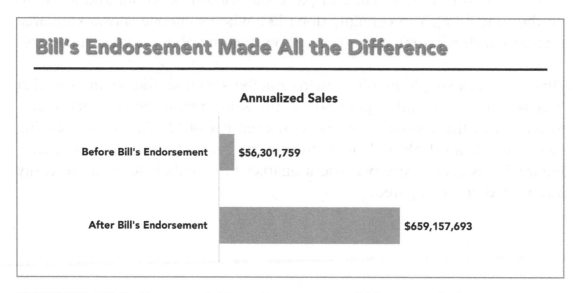

FIGURE 50B While Formatted, There Is More Detail Than Needed

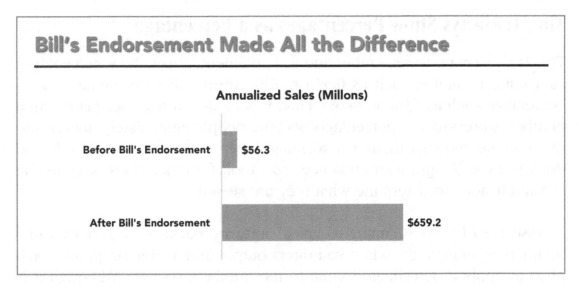

FIGURE 50C This Version Is Much Cleaner

Tip 51: Always Show Percentages as a Percentage

This is an easy tip to remember and to implement. *Never* show percentages as a regular number such as 0.53 or .746. Always show percentages as a percentage such as 53% or 74.6%. First, it is harder to read decimals than a number expressed as a percentage. Second, people immediately understand that you are showing them a percentage when you use the % sign. If you don't use the % sign, your audience must look for other clues, such as the column header, to determine what they are seeing.

As discussed in Tip 50, many technical software packages will output raw numbers by default. So, when you direct output into a table or graph, you'll need to apply a percentage format to the numbers yourself. Although it is simple to apply the format, it is very easy to cut and paste the software's output and forget to do the formatting. I see many presentations with percentages expressed as numbers and it bothers me every time.

One of the rare exceptions to this rule is in the financial world where interest rates or the difference between rates is often expressed in basis points instead of percentages.

Figure 51a shows a simple table with numbers used to represent the percentages. Notice how much easier it is to see the problem with the relationship between gifts and grades in Figure 51b even though the only difference is that the numbers are expressed as a percentage.

Something Looks Fishy

Student Segment	Percentage Getting an "A"	Percentage Getting an "F"
Honor Roll Students	.732	0.002
Frequently Sleep in Class	.295	0.471
Skipped Class Regularly	.153	0.893
Brought Bill Gifts	.999	0.000

FIGURE 51A The Table Is Hard to Read with This Format

Something Looks Fishy

Student Segment	Percentage Getting an "A"	Percentage Getting an "F"
Honor Roll Students	73.2%	0.2%
Frequently Sleep in Class	29.5%	47.1%
Skipped Class Regularly	15.3%	89.3%
Brought Bill Gifts	99.9%	0.0%

FIGURE 51B There Is Clearly a Problem with Bill's Gifts!

Tip 52: Provide Quantities *and* Percentages

Wouldn't you like to lessen the need to provide follow-up information to your audience? If so, then make it a point to always include quantities *and* percentages. For example, if you are asked to find the number of orders per store in your district, also show what percentage of orders each store represents. If you are asked to discuss total sales by product, also show the percentage of sales for each product. The reverse is also true. If you are asked what percentage of revenue each product represents, also include the total dollars.

Generally, whenever you are asked for either a quantity or a percentage, it is a good bet that there will also be interest in the one not explicitly asked for. Providing both is very easy and doing so provides additional information and context. Most analytical packages will default to providing counts or totals along with percentages. It is also trivial to compute one from the other. Therefore, default to always including both because there really is no excuse not to do it.

One risk with percentages is that due to rounding, your totals might be 99.9% or 100.1%. Some nontechnical audience members have trouble getting past this. So, consider forcing the percentages to exactly 100.0% by manually changing the rounding for a category that is very close to a 0.5% break.

Figure 52a is an example in which only the sales for each store is shown. It immediately leads to curiosity about what percentage those sales represent, doesn't it? Figure 52b shows sales and percentages. Unless you have a good reason to make an exception, mimic this approach because audiences will appreciate it and it will head off inevitable questions.

Suit Sales by Color

Suit Color	Total Atlanta Sales
Gray	$123k
Blue	$145k
Purple	$5k
Yellow	$2k

FIGURE 52A Don't You Want to See the Percentages Too?

Suit Sales by Color

Suit Color	Total Atlanta Sales	Percent Of Atlanta Sales
Gray	$123k	44.7%
Blue	$145k	52.7%
Purple	$5k	1.8%
Yellow	$2k	0.7%

FIGURE 52B The Percentages Make the Chart Much Better

Tip 53: Never Use Scientific Notation

Scientific notation has its place and can be quite helpful when dealing with huge numbers and complex math. One situation where scientific notation has no place is in a data-driven presentation . . . especially if delivered to a nontechnical audience. Scientific notation takes easy-to-understand numbers and makes them difficult to understand. If you need proof, just consider whether 12,345 is easier to understand than 1.2345E+04. Both express the same number, but the scientific notation format is just not intuitive.

A major reason that scientific notation makes its way into presentations is that some common software packages default to using scientific notation when creating charts and graphs. Why any software does this is beyond me. It makes no sense at all! So, someone requests a graph be created, their software creates a graph using scientific notation, and then the graph is pasted as is into a presentation. I don't think presenters typically use scientific notation by intentional design but rather through the laziness of just using what their software spits out by default.

I can't think of a single case where it would make sense to show scientific notation to an audience. If you are dealing with a lot of digits or decimals, state numbers in units of hundredths, thousandths, millions, billions, and so on as outlined in Tip 48. Leave scientific notation out of it!

Figure 53a is a basic graph using scientific notation, which makes it very hard to interpret. Figure 53b not only removes the scientific notation but also borrows from Tip 48 to simplify the graph even further.

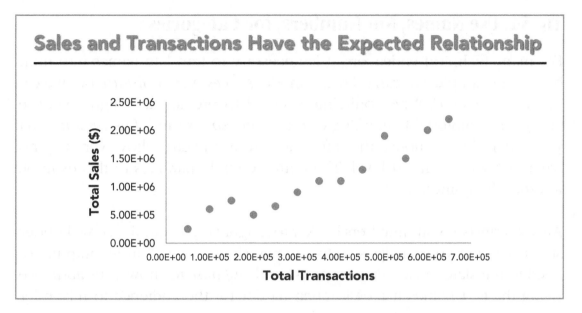

FIGURE 53A Scientific Notation Is Very Hard to Read

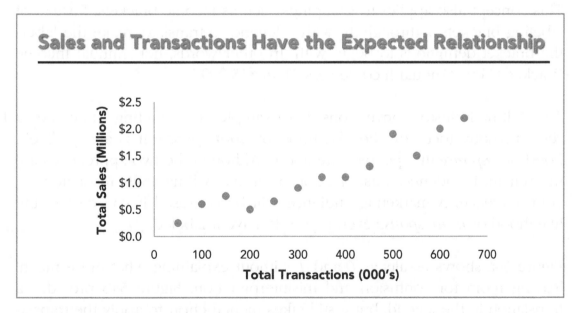

FIGURE 53B This Version Is Much Easier to Read

Tip 54: Use Names, Not Numbers, for Categories

For many technical endeavors, it is necessary to translate names into numbers. For example, we can't directly model *success* versus *failure* but we can model *1* versus *0*. When building a model to predict campaign response, you get so comfortable thinking of *0* as *nonresponse* and *1* as *response* that your brain doesn't notice the difference. Your audience, however, may not have that same comfort level. There are certainly parallels to this example in other disciplines.

Always translate your numbers back into language your audience will understand. Though your analysis software may show *0* and *1* in its output, you need to translate those to *nonresponse* and *response* to show your audience. Using the text names makes it much harder for the audience to misunderstand the information they are seeing.

This concept also applies to groupings such as income brackets. Instead of labeling brackets 1 through 10 with a legend to translate, make the labels the bracket definitions to begin with. In other words, not "Annual Income Bracket 1" but "Annual Income Less Than $15,000."

Also follow industry conventions. For example, in marketing I have never seen anybody focus on the likelihood of *nonresponse*. It is always likelihood of *response* that people care about. Although the two approaches are mathematically identical, use the approach that will naturally resonate with your audience. A marketing audience will be confused if you discuss the likelihood of *nonresponse* even if you do have it labeled.

Figure 54a shows results as *0* and *1* without explaining what those mean, leaving room for confusion and misinterpretation. Figure 54b provides a translation in the legend, but it still takes mental effort to apply the translation. Figure 54c makes the labels as clear as possible.

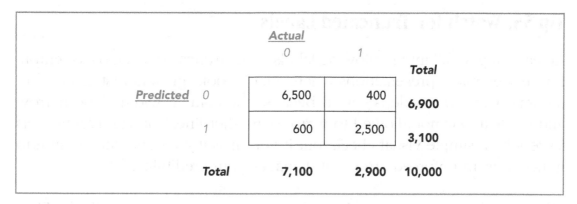

FIGURE 54A It Is Not Clear What "0" and "1" Mean

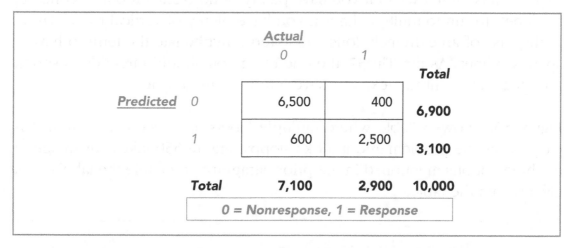

FIGURE 54B The Legend Helps, but Not Enough

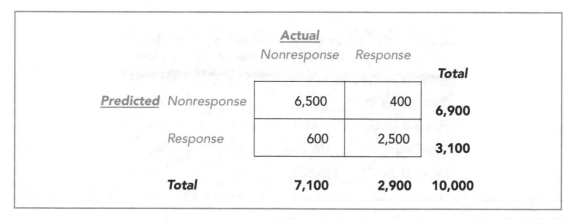

FIGURE 54C This Leaves No Room for Misinterpretation

Tip 55: Watch for Truncated Labels

An easy trap to fall into is allowing labels to get truncated in a table or graph. I have seen many presentations where a table looks great at first glance, but the text within the table is cut off because the column width is too narrow and the text was not allowed to wrap to another line. You can identify this issue with a simple visual check, but if you miss it your audience is sure to notice. It is an unforced error that damages your credibility.

When you have long descriptions, there are several options available. First, expand the column width if you have plenty of horizontal room. Second, let the labels to run to multiple lines if you have plenty of vertical room. Third, in the case of an extremely long single term, hyphenate the term to have it span two lines. As per Tip 37, the one thing you should rarely do is shrink your font size to fit the text you have into its current space.

Figure 55a shows a table where multiple labels have been truncated. It is easy to see the problem and it looks sloppy. Figure 55b takes advantage of all three options mentioned in the prior paragraph to enable the labels to fit cleanly into the table.

A Sampling of Famous Songs

Song	Good for Dancing?	Good to Annoy Neighbors?	Has Violent Themes?
Rapper's Delig	Yes	No	No
That Really Lon	No	No	Yes
Supercalifragili	No	Yes	No
Never Gonna G	Maybe?	Yes	No

FIGURE 55A Truncated Labels Ruin the Slide

A Sampling of Famous Songs

Song	Good for Dancing?	Good to Annoy Neighbors?	Has Violent Themes?
Rapper's Delight	Yes	No	No
That Really Long Speed Metal Song from the 90's	No	No	Yes
Supercalifragilisticexpiali-docious	No	Yes	No
Never Gonna Give You Up	Maybe	Yes	No

FIGURE 55B All Labels Made to Fit

Tip 56: Define All Acronyms and Abbreviations

There are commonly used acronyms, slang, or abbreviated terms that are used among coworkers or within an industry. These terms may not be familiar to those outside of a group. As a result, when presenting to anyone outside of your organization and/or technical discipline, spell them out in full. Always error on providing additional clarity for your audience. Tip 34 talks about including both plain language and technical terms when labeling data. It is also a good practice to follow that same model for acronyms and abbreviations.

There are acronyms that are common, such as EBITDA in finance (**E**arnings **B**efore **I**nterest, **T**axes, **D**epreciation, and **A**mortization). Most people have probably heard of EBITDA, but it would still be a good idea to include the full verbiage along with the common abbreviation. Because the abbreviation EBITDA is so common, some people might recognize the abbreviated form more than the spelled-out form. Showing both covers all the bases.

Figure 56a shows two options for defining EBITDA. One shows the acronym and the definition in the main body of the text. In the other, the definition is called out as a footnote. Although either option gets the job done, including both in the main body is preferable in cases where the audience is likely to be unfamiliar with the acronym. Using a footnote is preferable in cases where the audience is likely familiar with the acronym so that it doesn't add noise for those who don't need it.

- **Include the definition in the main text label**
  - *EBITDA (Earnings Before Interest, Taxes, Depreciation, and Amortization): $25.2 Million*

- **Include the definition as a footnote**
  - *EBITDA*: $25.2 Million*

  * Earnings Before Interest, Taxes, Depreciation, and Amortization

FIGURE 56A Two Options for Clarifying Acronyms

Tip 57: Use Dedicated Definitions Slides

We talk in Tip 33 about making sure your definitions are clear and in Tip 56 about using plain-language definitions. Sometimes, you will have a lot of terms in a presentation. Although that is perfectly fine, you must decide where to label and define the terms. This can be either on each specific slide or chart as demonstrated in other tips or on one or more slides dedicated to definitions, which we'll discuss here.

The options outlined in Tip 56 work great for one or two terms on a page, but they will get distracting and unwieldy if you have numerous terms. Too many labels on a chart can be almost as bad as too few. The best way to define a lot of terms is to have a definition slide (or slides) near the front of your presentation or in an appendix. Then, on each slide you can put a note at the bottom referring people to the definition page(s) if they desire clarity. This is also helpful for those who might read the presentation later because it allows each slide to stand on its own. It also avoids repetitive labeling of the same term again and again throughout the presentation.

The reason definitions are so important is that even seemingly simple terms such as *margin* or *sales* can be computed multiple ways within a large organization. Figure 57a shows a definitions slide that can either be placed early in the presentation to get the audience familiar with the terms they'll be hearing or be placed in an appendix for reference. It is also a best practice to verbally reinforce the definition of key terms as they appear during your live presentation.

- **Sales** – Total gross sales, excluding returns and employee purchases

- **Bill's Sales** – Total sales counting Bill's sales twice to make him look good

- **Margin** – Standard Finance team margin computed per policy 10.a.2.c.74

- **NPS** – Net Promoter Score. Percentage rating a product 8 - 10 minus the percent rating it 0 - 6. Our historical average is -72!

- **Adjusted Forecast** – Our best guess after consulting a psychic

FIGURE 57A An Example Definitions Slide

Tip 58: Clarify Aggregations Applied

There are often aggregations used for various purposes within a presentation. For example, you might show total sales by location on one slide and average sales by location on another. Yet another slide might show the maximum monthly sales by location. A common mistake is for a chart to just say *sales* in each of these situations instead of including the aggregation such as *average sales* or *total sales*.

For example, if the title of a slide is "Average Sales Per Month," then it isn't much of a stretch for someone to infer that the associated chart that simply says "Sales" represents average sales per month and not total sales. However, it also leaves open the possibility in the audience's minds that you meant to put average sales but accidentally included total sales instead. They are now questioning your attention to detail and credibility. The solution is to add the aggregation into the chart label as well. This is especially important if the chart itself gets passed around by itself without the slide's title to put it in context.

In Figure 58a, the chart is not clearly labeled and so there is doubt as to whether the chart matches the slide title or not. Figure 58b explicitly adds the aggregation label in the chart to provide clarity.

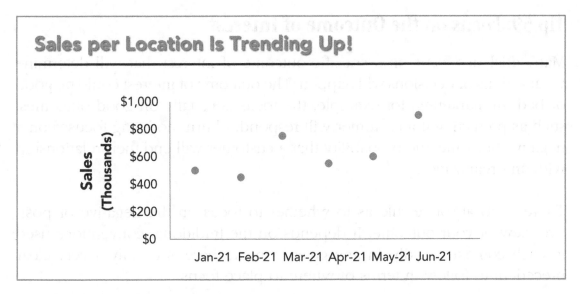

FIGURE 58A Ambiguous Axis Label

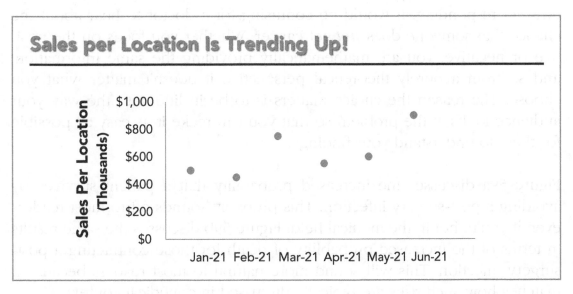

FIGURE 58B Clarified Axis Label

Tip 59: Focus on the Outcome of Interest

Many analytics focus on a specific outcome of interest that will determine what actions or decisions will happen. The outcome of interest could be good or bad. In marketing, for example, the focus is usually on good outcomes, such as predicting if a customer will respond. Churn modeling focuses on a negative outcome, the probability that a customer will end their relationship with an organization.

There is no absolute rule as to whether to focus on the negative or positive view of your outcome. It depends on the traditional conventions used in each context. Luckily, in any given context there is usually a very clear precedent to follow in terms of where to place focus.

It would be confusing for a marketer to hear about the probability of someone *not* responding. It would be confusing for a doctor to hear about the chance that someone does *not* get cancer. Whether you focus on the positive or negative, you are mathematically providing the same information, and so from a purely theoretical perspective it doesn't matter what you choose. The reason the choice matters is to be in line with the way your audience looks at the problem so that you can make it as easy as possible for them to understand your findings.

Figure 59a discusses the increased probability that a patient survives by avoiding a post-surgery infection. This probably sounds off to most readers even if you're not in the medical field. Figure 59b discusses the same results in terms of the increased probability of death for those contracting a post-surgery infection. This will sound more natural to most readers because it matches how such risks are typically discussed in a medical context.

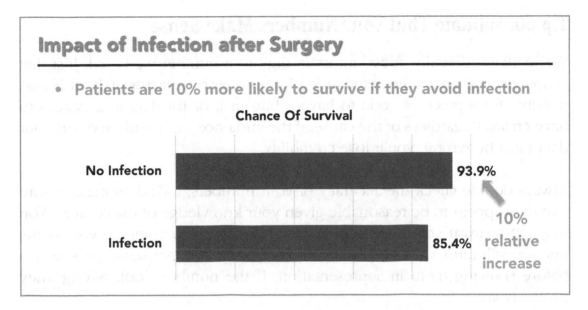

FIGURE 59A Chart Is Not Focused on the Outcome of Interest

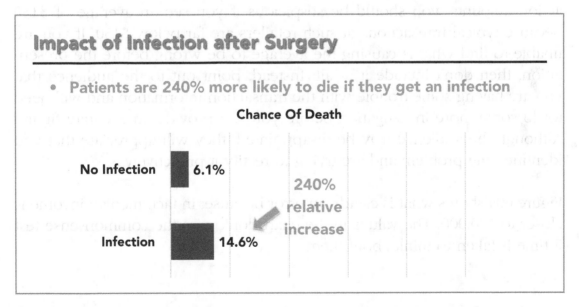

FIGURE 59B Chart Is Focused on the Outcome of Interest

Tip 60: Validate That Your Numbers Make Sense

We've all accidentally added an extra digit to a number we typed. Just that simple error changes the magnitude of a number by a factor of 10! It is also possible for a piece of code to have a bug in it or for data in a system to have errors. Regardless of the cause, if the audience can clearly see that your data must be wrong, you'll lose credibility.

Always double-check the accuracy of your numbers, including making sure that they appear to be reasonable given your knowledge of the context. You may not be aware of any system issues and may be confident in your code, but you still must validate your numbers from a commonsense perspective before showing them in a presentation. If the numbers look wrong, they probably are.

For example, if you are presenting information on convenience store transaction amounts, you should be suspicious if you see an average of $150 because typical transactions at such retailers are far below $150. If you are unable to find what is causing the average to be wrong before the presentation, then don't include it at all. Instead, point out to the audience that you are having some trouble with the transaction information and will need to do some more investigation before you can provide an accurate figure. Although the audience may be disappointed, they will appreciate that you identified the problem and are trying to rectify it proactively.

Figure 60a shows what is clearly an error because, in fact, median income is closer to $70,000. The values in the chart don't pass the commonsense test if time is taken to think about them.

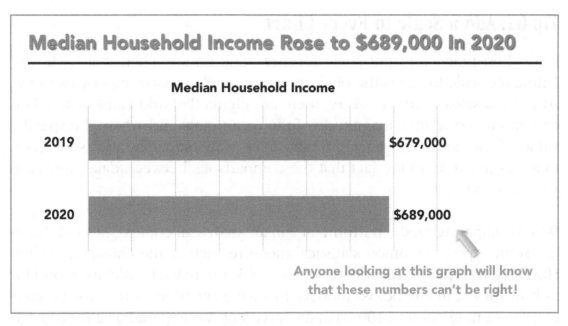

FIGURE 60A A Chart That Clearly Can't Be Correct

Tip 61: Add a Scale to Every Chart

It is a best practice to put some form of scale on any chart that is shown. Often, the scale to use is the obvious option, such as showing dollars as the scale for a sales chart. However, there are charts that add value only when comparing the relative magnitude of the data points and where the specific value of the numbers isn't important. Even in those cases, add something to alert the reader to the fact that the comparisons between data points are what is important.

When comparing model performance in an analytical context, it is helpful to use some type of common statistical measure such as the chi-square value. However, the specific magnitude of each chi-square isn't really as important as how they compare across models. In such a situation, you can scale your graph to a range of 0 to 100 so that everything is compared as a percentage of the largest. Even people who have no idea what a chi-square value is don't need to worry because the scale makes it clear they just need to see which option was best and by how wide a margin.

Figure 61a shows how scaling items to between 0% and 100% would look. By showing everything compared to the biggest data point (which gets a value of 100%), it helps make it clear to the audience that they should focus on the relationships between bars and not the specific values the bars represent.

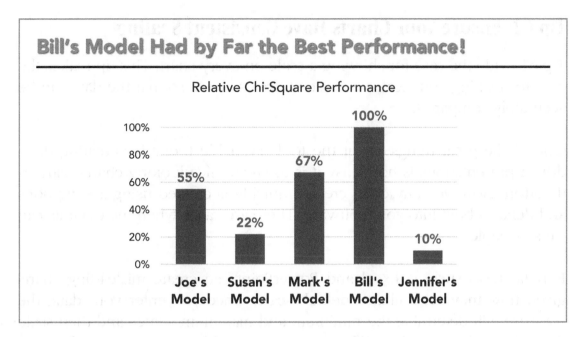

FIGURE 61A Data Scaled to Simplify Interpretation

Tip 62: Ensure Your Charts Have Consistent Scaling

Tip 61 made the case for showing a scale on every chart. This tip makes the case for making your scales consistent across charts so that the data can be accurately compared.

One of the great things about the tools available today for creating data-driven presentations is how easy it is to create nice-looking charts with little effort. However, any chart created quickly is created using assumptions and defaults built into your software. There are cases when the defaults can cause trouble.

Popular tools such as Excel and PowerPoint can create misleading charts given how they set a chart's default scale. Once you enter your data, the software will determine the minimum and maximum values and then scale the axis so that the chart fills the space available. An unintended consequence of this is that data of very different scales will look visually identical.

A graph showing a 25% difference between two response rates and a graph showing a 0.25% difference will look identical. The only way to know that the differences are 100× apart is by looking at the axis labels. To avoid ambiguity, be sure to show the axis labels so that the scale of the graphs is clear.

Figure 62a shows two graphs that look identical. This would lead a reader to think that the sales are identical for the two products. However, as Figure 62b shows, the sales for product B are one million times the sales for product A! This distinction is obvious with the scales shown in Figure 62b, whereas it was invisible in Figure 62a.

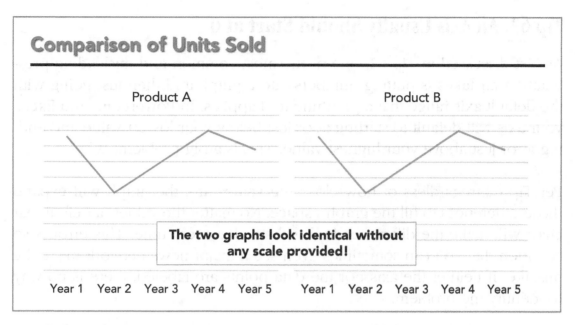

FIGURE 62A Graphs without Scale

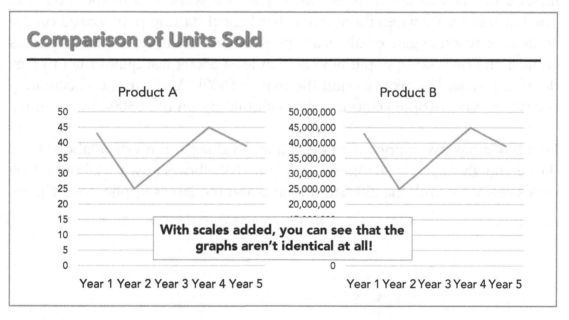

FIGURE 62B Graphs with Scale Added

Tip 63: An Axis Usually Should Start at 0

As just discussed in Tip 62, one of the most common and misleading presentation mistakes is putting numbers into a graph and then just going with the default axis range that a graphing tool applies. In PowerPoint and Excel, your axis will default to starting at or just below your lowest value and ending at or just above your highest value. This is a big problem. Why?

Per Tip 62, regardless of how close the values are, the graph will expand those differences to fill the graph's space. No matter the values, a default bar chart will make the difference look substantive every time. This error is so common that you can sometimes even see a major news network make the mistake. If neither the axis nor the data points are labeled, there is no way to identify the problem.

The simple solution is to always check your axis range and then always include the axis labels. In most cases, you will want to start the axis at 0. The exceptions are when there is another logical starting point based on the context or when negative values are present. For example, if there is a sales contest and only salespeople who sold at least $500k last quarter get to participate, it would be okay to start the axis at $500k. You can then accurately see where salespeople stand in terms of building on the $500k minimum.

Figure 63a has two graphs with default axis values and no data labels. Note the seemingly large visual difference. Figure 63b shows how trivial the differences really are with the axis starting at 0 and the labels applied per Tip 80.

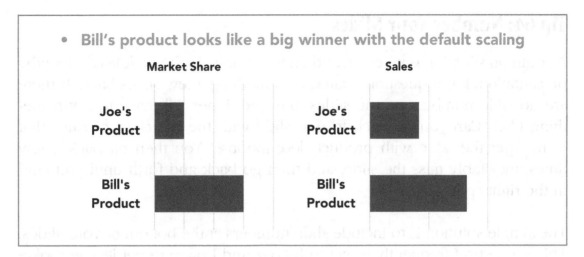

FIGURE 63A Comparison Using Default Axes

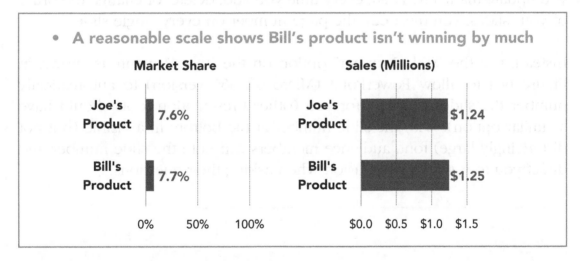

FIGURE 63B Comparison Starting Axes at 0

Tip 64: Number Your Slides

A common situation is when an audience member, in the middle of a lengthy presentation, has a question related to something a few slides back. If there are no slide numbers on the slides, the questioner will have to say something like, "Can you go back to that slide with the pie chart of sales that came after the table with product descriptions?" You then hit back a few times, inevitably miss the slide, and then go back and forth until you land in the right spot.

The simple solution is to include slide numbers at the bottom of your slides. This is one tip I frequently forget to follow, and I often regret it! The rookie mistake is to literally put a text box with a slide number on each slide that you update manually. Then, every time you add, delete, or change the order of your slides, you must edit the page number on every single slide.

Instead, use the "Slide Number" option on the "Insert" menu as shown in Figure 64a to allow PowerPoint (Microsoft 365 version) to automatically number the slides properly for you (other presentation tools should have a similar option). With the slide number at the bottom in a visible (but not distractingly large) font, audience members can note the slide number and direct you to it without confusion when asking their questions.

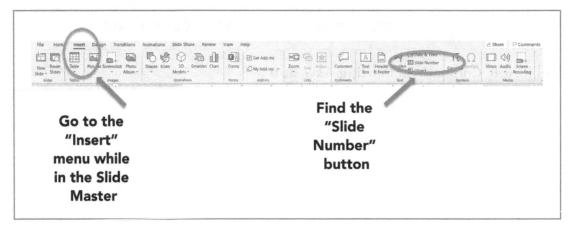

FIGURE 64A How to Add Slide Numbers

Developing: Charts, Images, and Layouts

The charts, tables, and imagery you incorporate into your data-driven presentation and how you organize them within your slides will have a large impact on your audience's perception of your presentation. The charts, tables, and imagery will also illustrate many of the most important messages that you intend to deliver as part of your story. As a result, it is well worth the effort to carefully consider what visuals to use, how to format them, and how to lay them out on your slides. Here are some of the concepts discussed in this section:

- Incorporate a mix of slide layouts to avoid repetitiveness.
- Shun highly technical or complex diagrams.
- Apply consistent formatting to tables and charts.
- Match colors to the context.
- Resist the urge to add advanced features to charts just because you can.

Once you accept the fact that you cannot take raw output from a technical software package and drop it into your presentation, you'll have no choice but to create your own charts, tables, and imagery to communicate the information you want to convey. After committing to creating charts and graphs, it doesn't take much incremental effort to ensure that you create and lay them out properly and in a way that will make your presentation look great while successfully communicating your core messages to the audience.

Developing Charts, Images, and Layouts

Tip 65: Use a Mix of Chart Types

Having a consistent look and feel to your presentation is good, but too much repetition can also be a bad thing. There are often options for the chart type you can use to effectively highlight any given critical point, so use a mix of chart types within and across slides to keep things fresh. Seeing the exact same style of bar chart over and over can be dulling to the senses of the audience.

Although you shouldn't use obscure chart types just for the sake of it (see Tips 68 and 69) or force data into a chart type that doesn't really match your need just for the sake of variety, you usually have the ability to add visual variety to your presentation. As discussed elsewhere, stick with specific fonts (Tip 39) and color palettes (Tip 72) and apply those to all of your charts. However, also apply them to a mix of chart types.

It can be particularly useful to mix chart types on a single slide when the data being shown isn't directly comparable from chart to chart, such as when you are displaying different metrics. Not only does using different chart types add variety to the slide but also it helps the audience see the distinct pieces of information instead of mentally trying to tie all the data directly together because it looks the same.

Figure 65a uses the same chart type repeatedly, which makes it hard to read and unappealing visually. Figure 65b uses several chart types, which helps focus attention on each chart individually while making the slide more visually appealing.

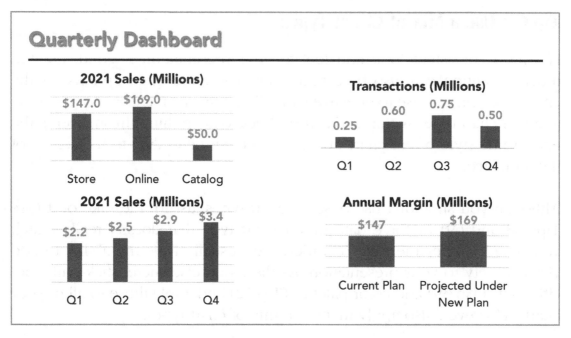

FIGURE 65A Too Many Charts of the Same Type Is Boring

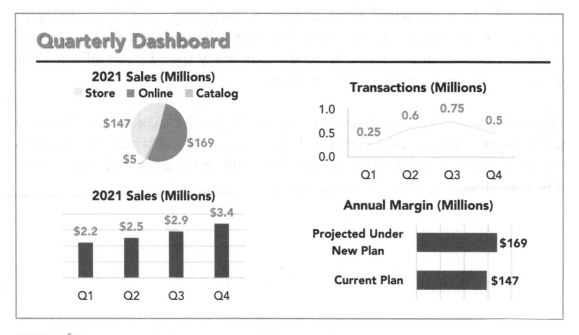

FIGURE 65B A Mix of Chart Types Adds Appeal

Tip 66: Use a Mix of Slide Layouts

Let's expand the concept discussed in Tip 65 to include slide layouts. Often, there are repetitive forms of information that must be shown during a data-driven presentation. A common example is a slide with a single chart or table, along with a comment. Once you have a slide layout that looks nice, it is tempting to use it over and over. This is good up to a point, but you should also consider mixing layouts.

For example, it is very common to place a chart on the left side of a slide with comments on the right. Instead of repeating that layout every time, mix in slides where the comments are on the left and the chart is on the right. You're still delivering the same information, but with a different visual look. The change in visuals can help draw the audience's attention back because their eyes will perceive that something is different.

I like to mix slide layouts in a somewhat random order. In other words, with 20 similar slides to show, alternating strictly between "chart on left" and "chart on right" will also become a predictable pattern to the audience. Flip back and forth enough to add variety, but not so that it is totally predictable. You can combine this approach with Tip 65 by also varying the chart type used in each slide layout.

Figure 66a illustrates a slide layout with the chart on the left and the text on the right while figure 66b illustrates a layout with the reverse. Same information, different look. Figure 66c shows how three layouts can be alternated to make repetitive content appear more dynamic.

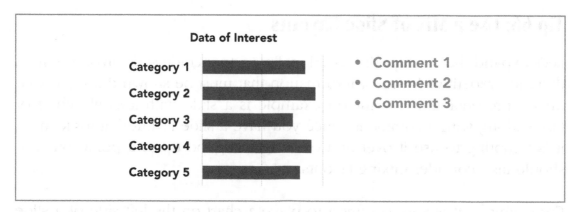

FIGURE 66A Layout with Graph on Left, Text on Right

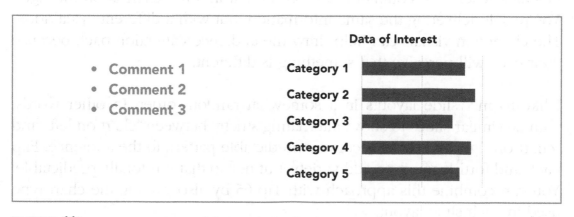

FIGURE 66B Layout with Graph on Right, Text on Left

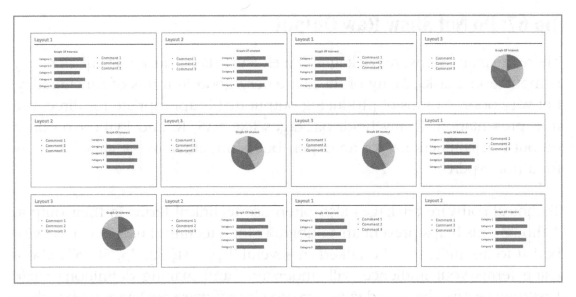

FIGURE 66C Alternating Layouts across Slides

Tip 67: Do Not Show Raw Output

There are many software packages that execute statistical, technical, or heavy computational tasks. Many of these are very good in terms of functionality, but very poor in terms of producing output that is appropriate for direct use in a presentation. In my field, packages like SAS, R, and Python produce output that is functional for an expert but is not attractive or easy to follow for a nonexpert.

Technical software packages also often use technical terms in their output. Although this helps prevent any ambiguity for a technical user, it can be gibberish to an audience. We talked in several Tips (31, 32, 33, 56, 57) about using terms your audience will understand and making definitions clear. Unattractive raw charts and tables created by software packages with technical terms the audience won't understand don't do that.

It is best to simply never use the raw, default output from technical software. Instead, take the output, identify the subsets worth showing, and create a nice-looking visual for your presentation that supports your story and guides the audience to action. It takes some extra work, but it ensures (1) a consistent look throughout your presentation, (2) only the necessary data is shared, and (3) your terminology is appropriate.

Figure 67a shows default output from SAS, a popular statistical package. It isn't the most visually appealing and the formatting of the numbers isn't ideal either. Figure 67b shows SAS output from a statistical model. It has a lot of great information for an expert, but most of the information should not be shown to an audience. Either create new visuals on your own or use the advanced formatting features of the software to make it format the output more nicely and succinctly on its own.

Frequency Percent Row Pct Col Pct	Table of product_group by product_region				
		product_region			
product_group	C1	C2	C3	NA	Total
B1	6886 0.63 58.19 1.48	788 0.07 6.66 0.35	2938 0.27 24.83 0.87	1221 0.11 10.32 2.12	11833 1.09
B2	748 0.07 51.59 0.16	296 0.03 20.41 0.13	329 0.03 22.69 0.10	77 0.01 5.31 0.13	1450 0.13
B3	322423 29.68 43.12 69.35	154444 14.22 20.66 67.96	237512 21.86 31.77 70.56	33281 3.06 4.45 57.75	747660 68.82
NA	134836 12.41 41.43 29.00	71714 6.60 22.04 31.56	95851 8.82 29.45 28.47	23053 2.12 7.08 40.00	325454 29.96
Total	464893 42.79	227242 20.92	336630 30.99	57632 5.30	1086397 100.00
Frequency Missing = 3417977					

FIGURE 67A Raw Output Example 1

Dependent Variable: height

Number of Observations Read	4504374
Number of Observations Used	1086397
Number of Observations with Missing Values	3417977

Analysis of Variance					
Source	DF	Sum of Squares	Mean Square	F Value	Pr > F
Model	2	2.065085E11	1.032542E11	19186.7	<.0001
Error	1.09E6	5.846489E12	5381555		
Corrected Total	1.09E6	6.052998E12			

Root MSE	2319.81795	R-Square	0.0341
Dependent Mean	686.78898	Adj R-Sq	0.0341
Coeff Var	337.77740		

Parameter Estimates					
Variable	DF	Parameter Estimate	Standard Error	t Value	Pr > |t|
Intercept	1	1340.11417	4.10535	326.43	<.0001
length	1	-38.03765	0.22003	-172.87	<.0001
width	1	5.90850	0.13624	43.37	<.0001

FIGURE 67B Raw Output Example 2

Tip 68: Keep It Simple

With so many chart types and chart options available in today's presentation software, it is possible to produce a multitude of chart versions with just a few clicks. However, there are many "fancy" options that look cool at first glance but are horrible options in practice. Keeping your charts simple and easy to interpret is your first goal, so follow the old adage of "keep it simple, stupid" or KISS. Only use unusual or advanced features when they explicitly assist in that goal.

Options that rarely add value include 3D features, multicolor gradients, or unusual fonts, among others. Although we discussed adding variety to your presentation in several tips, that variety should stay within the bounds of what the audience would consider to be typical and reasonable for the context in which you are presenting.

The chart on the left side of Figure 68a uses several unusual and fancy options that make the chart very hard to interpret. The chart on the right side of Figure 68a shows the same information with a typical format. Which do you think an audience would best be able to interpret? The chart on the right might seem boring compared to the chart on the left, but it is much more effective in conveying the information.

The goal when presenting data-driven content is to effectively convey information, not to win awards for artistic interpretation of data!

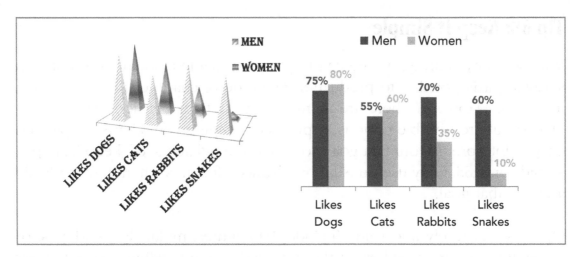

FIGURE 68A One Chart Is Clearly Better Than the Other!

Tip 69: Choose Charts That Are Easy to Interpret

One of the benefits of advances in computing power is the rise of visualization tools. In the early years of my work life, charts were literally created using standard text characters as seen in Figure 69a. This style of graphing forced people to keep things simple. Today, we have dozens of options at our fingertips for creating colorful, aesthetically pleasing graphs. This is a good thing, but it can be abused.

Love them or hate them, standard chart types like bar charts and line charts are familiar and easy to interpret for an audience. Don't use obscure chart types just because you can. Make sure that an unusual chart format has some specific value for your situation before using it. There are certain instances when a spider chart is a perfect fit, for example, but there are many more instances when a spider chart makes no sense. Choose the simplest, easiest-to-interpret chart that gets the job done.

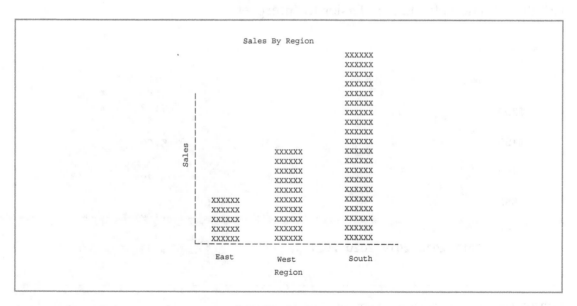

FIGURE 69A An Old School Graphic Made with Text

Figures 69b and 69c each show a standard chart format along with a less common format. The alternative formats are not very intuitive, and few people would suggest using them over the standard options shown in each figure.

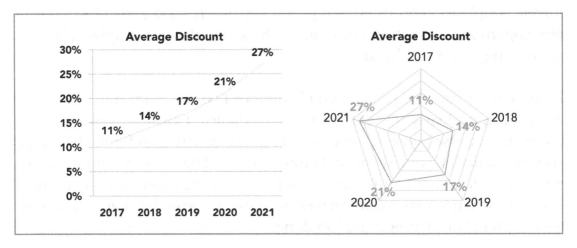

FIGURE 69B The Left Chart Is Easier to Interpret

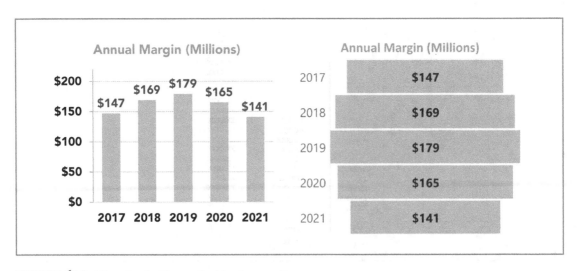

FIGURE 69C The Left Chart Is Easier to Interpret

Tip 70: Don't Show Incomprehensible Graphics

This is another tip that sounds obvious, but I routinely see presenters project a slide that is simply incomprehensible to their audience. Sometimes the terms on the chart are understandable, but the chart itself is too complicated for the audience to grasp. In Tip 7 we discussed that if you have to explain your chart, you've missed the mark. Even worse than that is when, even after your explanation, the audience still doesn't have a clue what you are talking about! It is like a joke people still don't get even after it is explained.

The most common cause of this error is when the presenter is highly familiar with certain information. It becomes second nature to the presenter and so they forget the audience does not deal with such things regularly (if ever).

Always look at your graphics through the eyes of your audience and make sure that the graphics will make sense to them. To mitigate your own biased view, ask a friend to review your graphics (see Tip 84). If your friend struggles to understand what you've created (especially after explanation), then you need to consider an alternate approach to presenting the information.

Figure 70a shows a chart like one I saw shown to a client. I honestly can't tell you what it was trying to show and neither could the audience. Although the presenter clearly thought it was important, the graphics and terminology used didn't get the point(s) across clearly.

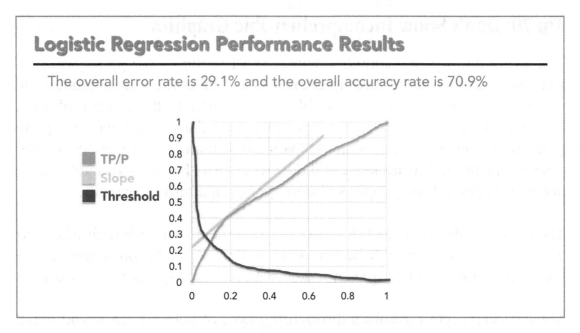

FIGURE 70A Most Audiences Would Not Understand This Graphic

Tip 71: Use Complex Graphics Strategically

There are times when a complex graphic can illustrate a critical part of the technical work you have done. Generally, a live presentation is not the occasion to show the details of such things because the audience is looking for key takeaways and potential actions, not complex details. The ability to absorb and comprehend complex graphics projected on a screen is minimal even for experts.

There is one exception to this rule, and that is when you want to briefly show some technical details just to prove that you have them. The goal isn't as much the audience's full comprehension of the content but audience recognition that you're discussing technically complex work. In this case, you strategically show the graphics quickly and explain that there is much more detail behind what you're discussing live.

This approach is specifically appropriate when technical people are also in the audience. They will be suspicious if you don't prove you have the detail. Show enough so the technical people can relax while sparing the nontechnical people the pain of hearing about it. Offer to provide the details in a written report or future discussion to those who desire them.

Figure 71a shows a decision tree. In a real situation, there would be even more text in each box, and it simply isn't readable on a screen. The goal of showing a tree like this is so that the audience can see the depth and complexity of the tree, not the individual cell descriptions. Figure 71b removes the text so that the audience is forced to focus only on the shape. The complexity is clear while nobody can get lost in the details because the details aren't shown!

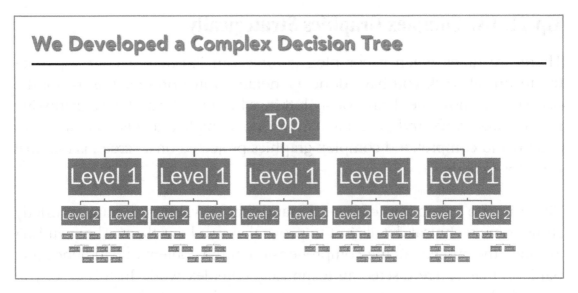

FIGURE 71A This Graphic Is Too Detailed

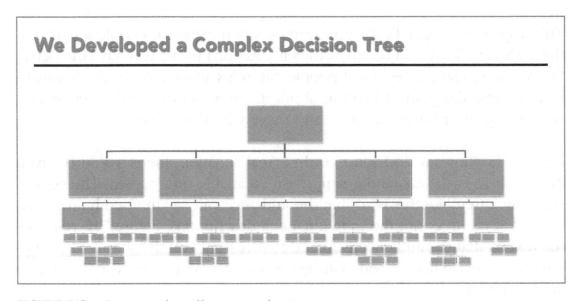

FIGURE 71B This Graphic Illustrates the Tree's Structure

Tip 72: Coordinate Your Colors

Just like a color-coordinated outfit looks nice on a person, the color combinations used in a presentation can add to (or detract from!) its visual appeal. Using colors that are compatible and complementary is so important that tools such as PowerPoint provide the ability to choose a prespecified palette for use in your presentation. (See the "Colors" tab under "Slide Master" per Figure 72a, which is based on the Microsoft 365 version.)

We won't delve into the depths of how to choose color palettes from an aesthetics perspective. Rather, we'll focus on a basic guideline that will help you avoid the most common pitfalls. The simple guideline is to ensure that your text and graphics are visible when layered. If some in your audience are color-blind, you can also consider using patterns instead of colors and/or choosing colors that color-blind people can see.

Black text on a dark gray background can be nearly impossible to see, as can orange text on a yellow background. As you develop your slides, keep an eye out for situations where you inadvertently create a hard-to-see visual. For example, a bar chart with 10 bars requires 10 colors. Those that PowerPoint automatically applies may or may not each be compatible with your text color, and you may have to apply some manual overrides.

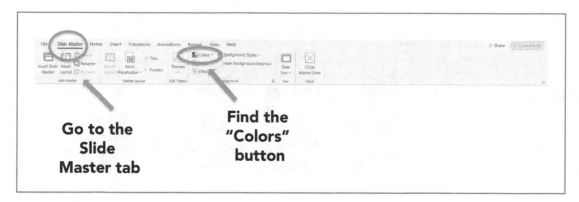

FIGURE 72A How to Apply a Consistent Color Palette

Figure 72b shows a slide with several bad color combinations. Figure 72c has made corrections to fix the issues. Note that although you usually want to keep your fonts and colorings consistent, it is okay to use a different text color in places where the default font can't be properly seen, as was done for Product A in Figure 72c.

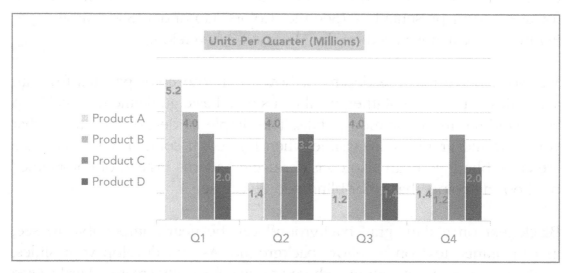

FIGURE 72B These Color Combinations Are Difficult to Read

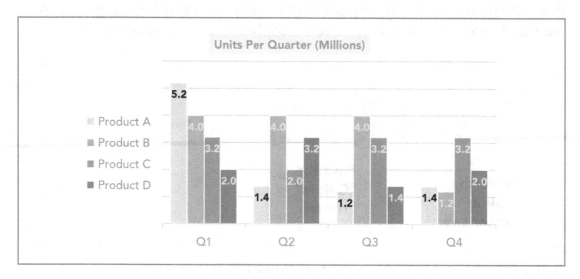

FIGURE 72C These Color Combinations Are Easier to Read

Tip 73: Keep Colors in Context

Another important consideration when choosing colors for your slides is to make sure that your colors are chosen in context of what you are discussing and who you are discussing it with. There are multiple ways the need for this concept can manifest itself.

When presenting to an organization, be sensitive to the colors that the organization uses. For example, Coca-Cola is famously red while Pepsi is famously blue. Showing up at Pepsi with a red palette is going to go over very poorly! Similarly, if presenting to a sports team, you should use the team's jersey colors (or at minimum avoid using the colors of their rivals).

When showing gains and losses or positive metrics and negative metrics, tradition says that green is good and red is bad. Having slides that show good news in red will cause cognitive dissonance in your audience's mind; they'll wonder why you broke convention, and it will harm your credibility. Figure 73a has a basic table with the positive figure in red and the negative figures in green. It just looks wrong. Figure 73b has the colors reversed and looks more natural.

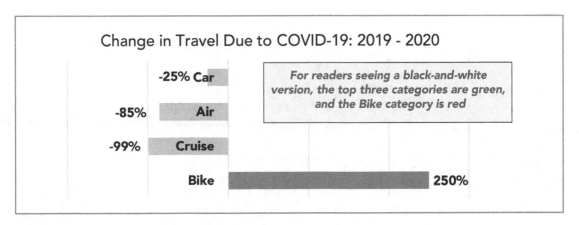

FIGURE 73A It Looks Odd for Negative Numbers to Be Green

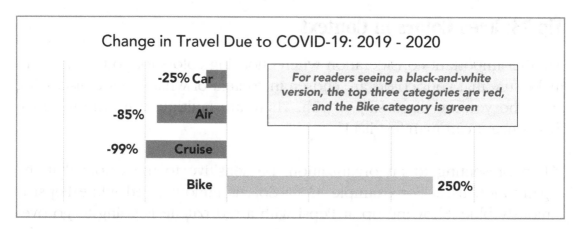

FIGURE 73B Coloring Negative Numbers Red Looks "Normal"

There are also situations when certain colors are historically tied to certain categories. For example, in the United States, Democrats are blue and Republicans are red. Similarly, blue is used for baby boys and pink for baby girls. Break such conventions in your presentation at your own risk!

Tip 74: Shun Technical and Architectural Diagrams

Technical people love to show technical diagrams. One place that this is rampant is in the information technology (IT) field. Systems architecture diagrams are shown frequently in IT-related meetings even though most of the audience doesn't know what many of the components of the architecture are, let alone how they all connect. Seeing a complex systems architecture diagram doesn't help educate nontechnical audiences as much as it lets the presenter show the audience how complex the presenter's world is (by the way, the audience doesn't care how complex the presenter's world is!).

As a rule, do not show systems architecture or similar technical diagrams if you aren't presenting to a technical audience. Presenting such information will reinforce the common audience presumption that you are "too technical" to help them in a practical way. It will take you far too long to try and explain the diagram, even though it is almost certain your explanation will fail. It will confuse the audience and cause them to shift focus from your story to their social media or emails. Avoid these issues by resisting the urge, no matter how strong, to show technical diagrams. If you feel compelled to include them somewhere, put them in an appendix.

Regardless of how pretty your technical diagram is and how proud you are of it, the reality is that what your audience sees is what is in Figure 74a. Unfortunately, to a nontechnical audience your favorite technical diagram is just a bunch of meaningless icons and arrows on a page. If you stop to consider how your diagram looks through the audience's eyes, it is easy to see why it isn't a good idea to present it.

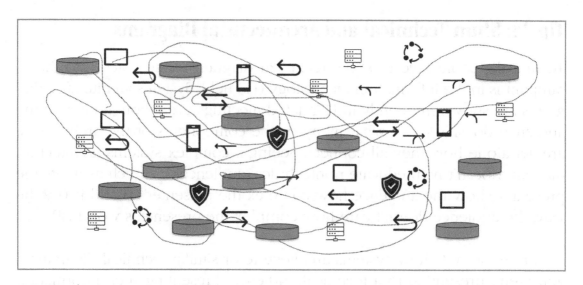

FIGURE 74A Architecture Diagram: What a Non-Technical Audience Sees

Tip 75: Don't Let Accent Graphics Steal the Show

Accent graphics are images that don't explicitly show data or information but that add a little flair to your data-driven presentation. I am a big fan of accent graphics! If presenting to a soft drink manufacturer, for example, you might include pictures of their products throughout. If presenting to a clothing manufacturer, you might have images of their clothes. If presenting to a retailer, you might have images of their stores. In all those cases, the accent graphics will help tie your results to the brand.

It is also acceptable to use accent graphics that are more conceptual. If discussing a common frustration, you might have an image of a person who is frustrated. If discussing a risky decision, you might show someone bungee jumping. If discussing a big win, you might show a picture of a sports team celebrating. In these cases, conceptual accent graphics are used to break up the monotony of slide after slide of text, tables, graphs, and charts.

Accent graphics should be just that . . . an accent, however, and should not be front and center such that they are the focus of your slide. Rather, they should blend into the slide and augment the key facts and figures shown. It is easy to get carried away and add too many accent graphics so that a slide is crowded or to make an accent graphic so large that it visually dominates, so be cautious with them.

Figure 75a illustrates an accent graphic that is much too large. It dominates the slide. Figure 75b shrinks the accent graphic and makes it blend in nicely next to the data.

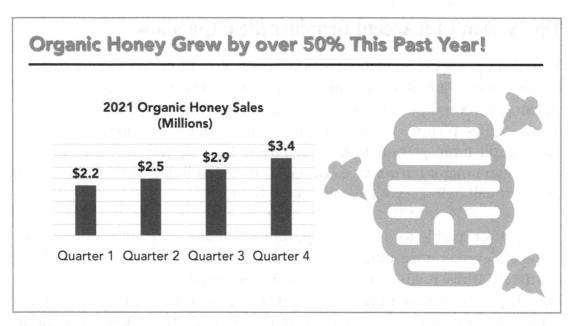

FIGURE 75A A Dominating Accent Graphic

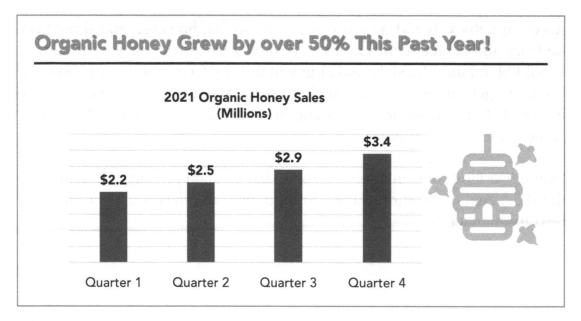

FIGURE 75B An Accent Graphic That Blends In

Tip 76: Format Tables Consistently

A repeated theme in this book (see Tips 35, 39, 62, and 72) is that consistency of approach is a good thing in a data-driven presentation. This also applies to the way that you format any data tables that you choose to present. If you prefer to alternatively shade rows to help the eye separate them, then do that throughout your presentation. If you are going to make your totals bold and underlined, then do that consistently throughout your presentation. Consistency across multiple tables on a single slide is even more important than consistency across slides, so rarely use multiple formats within a single slide.

Do not worry about what the "best" format is as much as you worry about choosing a format and sticking with it. The audience will have an easier time following your story if their eyes and minds get used to seeing information in a certain way. Consistently using the third-best format will be more effective than randomly alternating between many formats.

Figure 76a shows several tables that are all formatted differently. It makes it harder to absorb the information and doesn't look appealing. In Figure 76b, all the tables are consistently formatted. Notice how much nicer the slide looks while also making it easier for you to comprehend the numbers presented.

Profile of Students Getting an A In Bill's Class

Gift Status	
Gave Bill Gifts	92%
Did Not Give Bill Gifts	8%

Student Average GPA	
In Major Courses	3.8
Out-of-Major Courses	3.5
Overall GPA	3.65

Extra Support per Student

Total Tutoring Expenses	$550
Total Past Exam Purchases	$75
Total	$625

Degree Program	
Data Science Major	85%
All Other Majors	15%

FIGURE 76A Inconsistent Formats Are Distracting

Profile of Students Getting an A In Bill's Class

Gift Status	
Gave Bill Gifts	92%
Did Not Give Bill Gifts	8%

Student Average GPA	
In Major Courses	3.8
Out-of-Major Courses	3.5
Overall GPA	3.7

Extra Support per Student	
Total Tutoring Expenses	$550
Total Past Exam Purchases	$75
Total	$625

Degree Program	
Data Science Major	85%
All Other Majors	15%

FIGURE 76B Consistent Formats Look Cleaner

Tip 77: Use Shading to Make Tables Easily Readable

The more information you put on a slide, the harder it is for the audience to consume it while you are speaking. There are situations when you may not be able to avoid showing a table with multiple rows and columns. When you determine that you must show a bigger data table, use some simple methods to make it easily readable. Note, however, that your first choice (per Tip 22) should be to create several slides that drill down on a few of the numbers at a time to make the presentation as easy to follow as possible.

If you show a large table, follow these simple rules. First, using shading and bold letters to make your header row stand out. Second, alternate a lighter and darker shade of coloring to make the rows easier to distinguish. Third, make sure your font is big enough to see and has coloring that makes it readable when placed on top of the row shading you choose.

Figure 77a shows a table that is all one color, with no lines separating any of the cells, and no bolding. Figure 77b shows the same table with some coloring, lines, and bolding to make it easier to focus on specific parts of the table. Again, it might be better to have this full table in an appendix and have smaller tables or charts that focus just on specific points you want to make.

Fabricated Metrics for Male High School Athletes

Measure	Baseball	Basketball	Football	Soccer	Tennis	Track
Height	5'10"	6'4"	6'1"	5'11"	5'10"	5'9"
Weight	175	200	225	165	165	160
Plays in Elite Private League	60%	65%	40%	75%	40%	5%
Plays for High School Team	75%	71%	87%	70%	91%	95%
Uses Personal Trainer	21%	17%	35%	15%	30%	10%
Plans to Play in College	9%	5%	6%	7%	3%	10%

FIGURE 77A Table without Shading

Fabricated Metrics for Male High School Athletes

Measure	Baseball	Basketball	Football	Soccer	Tennis	Track
Height	5'10"	6'4"	6'1"	5'11"	5'10"	5'9"
Weight	175	200	225	165	165	160
Plays in Elite Private League	60%	65%	40%	75%	40%	5%
Plays for High School Team	75%	71%	87%	70%	91%	95%
Uses Personal Trainer	21%	17%	35%	15%	30%	10%
Plans to Play in College	9%	5%	6%	7%	3%	10%

FIGURE 77B Table with Shading

Tip 78: Don't Put Borders Around Charts

It seems reasonable to assume that putting a border around tables and charts would help an audience to more clearly separate components of your slide from each other. In practice, however, borders make a slide look busier and more complex. You may not have noticed, but in all but a few places in this book the example tables and charts do not have borders. That is not a coincidence!

As with any rule, there are exceptions. The tables you saw in Figure 76b, for example, do have a border. In this case an exception was made because the tables are small and similar in size, so the borders help separate them. However, that is a rare exception. Usually, a border will make a slide look worse, not better. Tables are also more likely to warrant an exception to this rule than charts.

Counterintuitively, the more graphics you have on your slide, the less likely you want to use borders. If your slide is so busy that you think your graphics need borders to help delineate them from each other, then you need to break the slide into multiple slides of lesser complexity instead of adding borders.

Figure 78a takes the content from Figure 80b and adds borders around the graphics. It looks notably less appealing. Figure 78b takes the content from Figure 65b and does the same. The chart looks worse than the original.

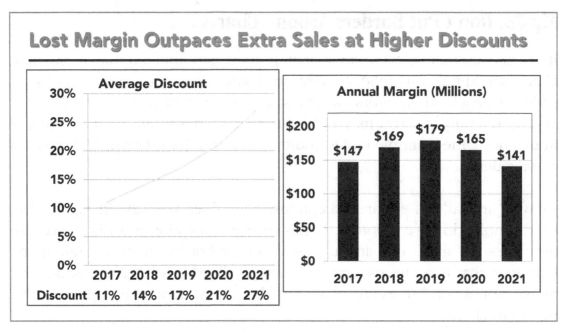

FIGURE 78A Chart Borders Usually Look Bad

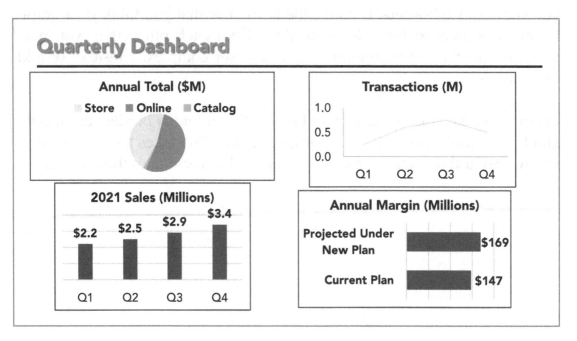

FIGURE 78B Chart Borders Usually Look Bad

Tip 79: Limit the Number of Categories

When there are a lot of products, geographies, time frames, or other categorical groupings, a natural inclination is to want to show the audience all of them. This works great when you have a handful of categories, but not when there are many. When there are many categories, the table or graph will be cluttered and it will be hard for the audience to interpret your information.

The primary way to handle a large number of categories is to show a handful and combine the rest into an "All Other" category. That way, you've accounted for everything, but in a way that is easier on the eyes. Usually only the largest categories are of interest anyway, so you don't really lose anything.

The most common way to create an "All Other" category is to keep the top 5–10 categories and then combine all of the smaller ones together. You can safely include more categories in a text table than a chart. Sometimes there are categories of specific interest regardless of their prevalence. In that case, it is fine to show some specific smaller categories while still combining the rest. If necessary, have an appendix that shows each of the components of the "All Other" category individually.

Figure 79a includes a pie chart with too many categories included. It looks bad and it is hard to see the smaller categories cleanly. Figure 79b shows the top five along with an "All Other" category and is much easier to read and interpret.

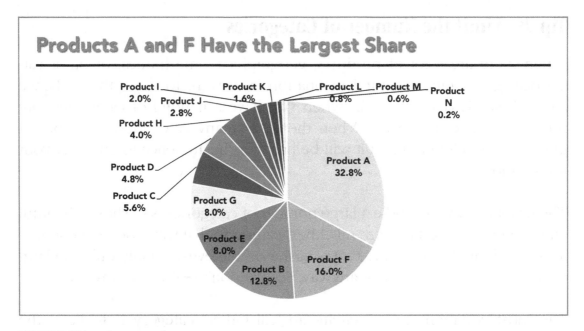

FIGURE 79A Chart with Too Many Categories

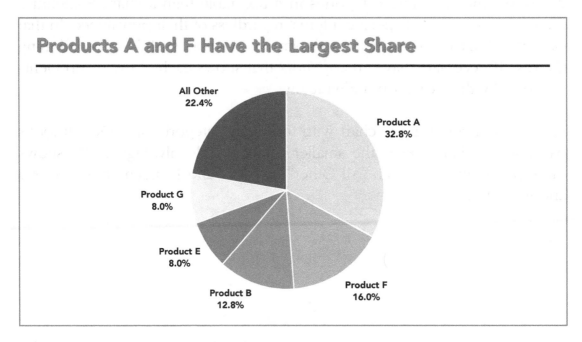

FIGURE 79B Chart with an "All Other" Category

Tip 80: Label Your Data

Most people will want to know the exact value of any given point or bar in a chart, and so it is safest to include the value labels as your default practice. On the occasions you don't include the labels, Murphy's Law says that someone in the audience will ask you what the values are!

There are two options for providing the values. The first is to show the values above or on top of the various bars and points. Common charts have this as a standard option. The second is to have a table with the data below the chart. Adding a data table is also a standard option for most charts, so you don't even have to create a separate table if you don't want to.

Figure 80a shows two charts that do not have values included, which makes them nice and simple, but also leaves the audience wondering exactly what the values are. Although the axis labels provide a way to estimate the values,

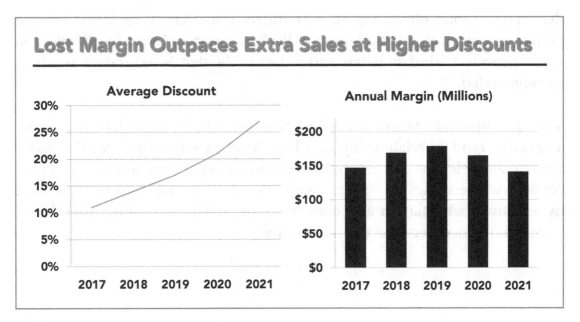

FIGURE 80A Data Labels Not Shown

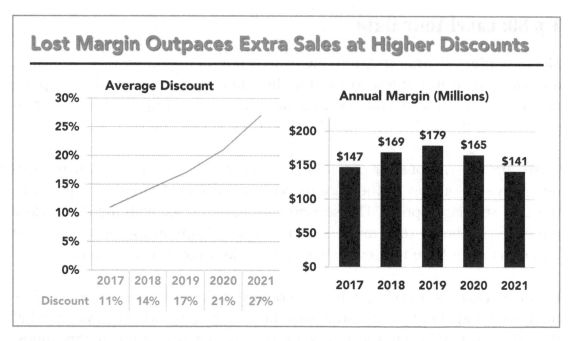

FIGURE 80B Data Labels Included

that takes mental effort. Figure 80b shows one chart with labels on the graph and one with a table below it. Both are more informative. While you could provide both data labels and a data table, that is redundant and isn't recommended.

You can sometimes violate this rule when the point of your chart is to show a specific trend or relationship at a high level or when the specific values aren't really relevant. For example, a graph showing how inflation has outpaced costs increases for several years. People don't need to be distracted by exactly what inflation and costs were as much as grasping the clearly visible difference between them over time.

Tip 81: Avoid Stacked Bar Charts

Many people love to use stacked bar charts. I absolutely hate them. The reason is that the only category you can accurately compare in a stacked chart is the first one. After that, the starting points of the other categories are offset from each other, and that makes it very hard to compare them. The more categories, the worse it gets as you move up the axis. With enough categories, you can literally end up with one bar having a category's starting point above another bar's ending point for the category. The same is true whether stacking percentages or totals.

If the only thing that matters is the total that the stacked pieces add to, then just show the total as a bar and don't show the stacked categories at all. If the individual pieces matter, then present them in a format that makes it easy to see and compare the pieces, such as a clustered column chart.

Figure 81a shows a stacked chart. Notice how hard it is to compare anything except the bottommost category. The final category at the top doesn't overlap

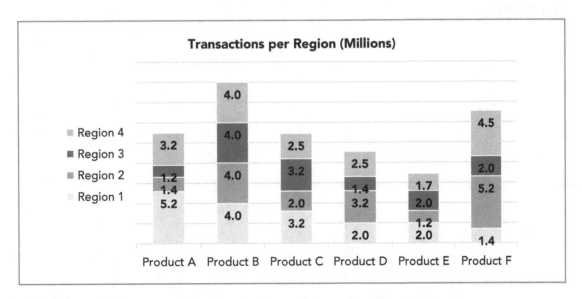

FIGURE 81A It Is Very Hard to Compare All but the First Region

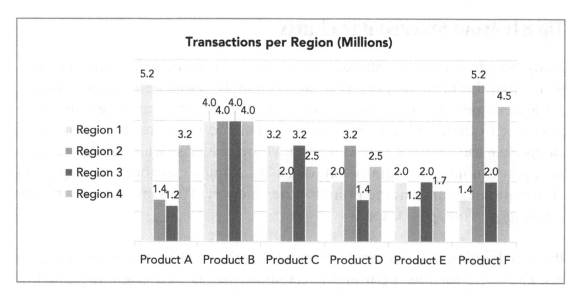

FIGURE 81B It Is Much Easier to Compare the Regions by Product

at all for some bars, which makes it even harder to compare. Figure 81b shows the same information as a clustered column chart. It is much easier to see how the categories compare using that format, though even this chart is a bit busy.

Tip 82: Put the Cause on the *X*-Axis

Oftentimes, a scatterplot is used to show how one factor is associated with another. Sometimes, there is a true cause-and-effect relationship and sometimes there is not. When there is a potential cause-and-effect relationship, standard practice is to put the cause on the horizontal, or *x*-axis. Not following that practice will throw your audience off.

Even if you are not attempting to make a case for cause and effect, sometimes there is a logical orientation anyway. For example, height does not directly cause weight. But, it is more logical to think about more height causing someone to become heavier than more weight causing someone to become taller. So, put height on the *x*-axis.

Consider the average calorie intake per day compared to weight gain. More calories will lead to more weight, but weight gain doesn't cause you to eat more calories! Figure 82a has weight gain on the *x*-axis and calories on the *y*-axis. It will strike most readers as odd because usually such a graph will have the cause, or daily calories, on the *x*-axis as in Figure 82b. Figure 82b looks more natural.

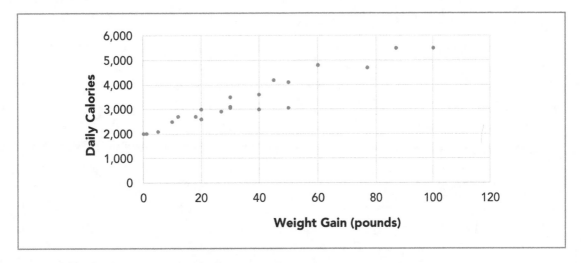

FIGURE 82A This Layout Implies Weight Gain Causes Daily Calories

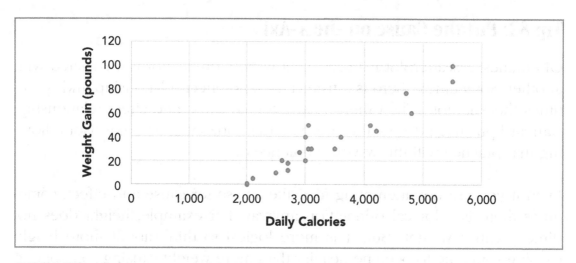

FIGURE 82B This Layout Implies Daily Calories Cause Weight Gain

Delivering: Final Presentation Preparation

After you've developed your data-driven presentation content, you must prepare for and practice your delivery. Knowing what you'll say, anticipating the questions you'll receive, and validating that your spoken words flow smoothly are critical to success. Without proper preparation, you risk having all of your previous work be for naught. Here are some of the concepts discussed in this section:

- Consult a confidant and/or sponsor.
- Adapt your presentation to the audience.
- Be prepared to cut your presentation substantively short.
- Have multiple backup plans for handling problems that can arise.
- Ensure your key points are clear and that you draw attention to the right places.

Your final preparation is the last chance to ensure your messaging is on target, your slides are easy to follow, and that you're able to successfully drive home the points that you want to make. During final preparations, you'll always find some fine-tuning that will make your presentation better as well as spots where you need to make your verbiage clearer and crisper. Most important, you can identify where your content is strongest (and weakest) and adjust your presentation flow for maximum effect.

Tip 83: Practice Your Presentation

You won't know how long your presentation will take without practice runs. Next time you have a presentation ready but have not yet delivered it, make an estimate of how long it will be. You'll almost certainly be off, and often by a sizable percentage. You can get away with finishing a presentation faster than estimated, but if you're slower than estimated, you'll run short of time and will either not complete your presentation or will have to move too quickly to finish it properly.

In addition to validating your timing, forcing yourself to go through your presentation will enable you to tune your flow by identifying where you are smooth, where you struggle, what content seems stronger and weaker than you expected, and where you might have too much redundancy or technical detail. I have had many occasions where I thought my flow was solid, but during a dry run I realized that it needed some changes. I also routinely find places where I struggle for the words to get my point across. I then focus time on tuning those sections of my narrative.

Some people resist the idea of a practice presentation because it can seem silly to be in a room by yourself presenting. However, think about written documents. Does anyone you know send out a written document that is the first draft with no further review? No way. Everyone understands that multiple passes of edits are required to get a document to the level it needs to be. Why would a live presentation be any different? You may be speaking instead of writing, but it is still about getting the right words in the right order to deliver your message clearly and concisely. Many people will make multiple rounds of edits to their slides, but somehow don't think to also do multiple passes of what they will say to support those slides. If presenting by yourself is too uncomfortable, invite a friend or two to sit in and offer feedback (see Tip 84).

If you have presented material multiple times and are comfortable with it, you may not need to do a full practice run because your prior presentations serve that purpose. You might still do a quick pass as a refresher, however. In my work, I have developed literally thousands of slides on different topics. I keep a log of approximately how long each one takes, and that enables me to estimate the length of a new combination of slides fairly accurately even without a practice run. However, if I haven't used certain slides in a while, I'll still do a practice run of them to refresh myself with how to speak to each slide. I also always time out new slides as soon as I create them.

If you aren't yet used to speaking to a live audience, you can hone your skills further by making a video of a practice run. Ideally, you should video yourself in the environment in which you'll be presenting, whether in a conference room, on a stage, or over a virtual platform. Watch your video and you'll see all sorts of things you'll wish you hadn't. You may find you're speaking too softly (it is almost impossible to speak too loudly in most presentation environments), or that you're speaking too quickly, or that you're looking at your notes too much, or that you keep scratching your head. Seeing and hearing yourself as the audience does is a great way to spot ways to improve your presentation mechanics.

Tip 84: Consult Some Confidants

No matter how diligent you are when putting together your data-driven presentation, you will always miss something. You may have blind spots that are causing you to neglect making a key connection between findings. You may have developed a flow that is distracting you from optimally communicating your message. One of your points might be of no practical interest to your audience, though you aren't aware of that fact.

One great way to identify such issues is to consult with one or more confidants as you make final preparations for your presentation. By providing a preview to friendly outsiders, you get the honest feedback you need to help flag the areas of the presentation that need more work. Especially for a high-stakes presentation, it is incredibly risky for you to go into the room having never gone through the presentation for anyone but yourself or your core project team. There are two types of confidants to consider pulling into the process.

First is someone from your extended team who is totally familiar with the type of project you executed and the methodologies that you made use of, but who is not familiar with the specifics of your project. Such a confidant can catch technical inconsistencies or gaps by bringing fresh eyes and expertise to the table.

Second is someone from the project's sponsoring organization, whether an internal business unit or an external company. This is someone you trust, but who does not have expertise related to your project. Such a confidant will help identify areas that are confusing or unclear to a nonexpert audience. Most important, they can validate that the way you are positioning the findings and recommendations will, in fact, resonate with the audience for which it is intended.

In the consulting world, we always look for an *inside coach* at a client who is friendly to our cause and who is willing to help ensure that we hit the mark so that we can provide the most benefit to the coach's organization. It is impossible to overstate how important candid feedback from someone who intimately understands your audience is. An inside coach will know things that you don't know about the audience and project politics and will be able to help you tighten up your narrative and approach.

Of course, consulting confidants will take time. Even more time will be required to make the adjustments that are suggested by the confidants. You can't leave it to the last minute. Per Tip 10, you must place time in your budget up-front or you risk not having time to consult with your confidants as your presentation nears. Prevent that from happening!

Tip 85: Don't Overprepare

It sounds odd to say that it is possible to overprepare for a data-driven presentation, but it is. We just discussed in Tips 83 and 84 how critical it is to prepare. We'll discuss in Tip 101 how damaging it can be to read your slides. Only a single step up from reading slides is when your presentation is so rehearsed and so well memorized that it makes you sound dull and monotone. Preparation is critical, but it really is possible to overdo it.

You certainly want to spend time rehearsing what you'll say, but only take rehearsing so far. I create a few bullets for myself related to each slide. These bullets will remind me of the main points I need to make on that slide. Instead of scripting my narrative verbatim, I purposely keep it to a couple bullet points. Of course, to discuss those bullet points will require many more words. By not scripting my words for each point, I am forced to verbalize my points on the fly in terms of the specific phrasing I use to make each point. Although every iteration of my presentation will be slightly different, it will sound more natural, authentic, and conversational to the audience.

Even with bullets, you can rehearse so much that you're still reciting more than speaking. Find the sweet spot where you know your material well enough that you generally know what to say for each slide. Then, stop there and trust that when the time comes, you'll say something consistent enough to succeed.

If you are so uncomfortable without a script that you feel that you absolutely must use one, then the lesser evil is to use the script. This is preferable to stumbling or losing your place repeatedly if you are not able to explain your points on the fly. But make it a goal to get better at going without a script. Pay attention to speakers at meetings you attend, and I promise that you will easily tell who is reading a script and who is just talking. It is very easy to tell the difference even if you close your eyes so you can't see the person looking at their notes. You can absolutely hear the difference. Hearing that difference will motivate you to avoid fully scripting your presentations.

Tip 86: Adjust Your Story to the Audience

You've just pulled together a crisp, focused presentation and story for your meeting with the marketing team when you are asked to present to the finance team next week. The good news is that you can take your presentation and story to the next meeting as is, right? Wrong! The marketing team will be interested in how they can leverage your findings to improve their message, targeting, segmentation, and so on. However, the finance team will want to know what this will mean to investment ROI and future revenues. Unfortunately, the right presentation for one audience might not be the right presentation for another. Per Tip 5, you must know each audience and adjust your delivery accordingly.

My friend Brent Dykes gave a great example of this concept in his book *Effective Data Storytelling* (Wiley, 2020). I will provide my own version of his example here. Consider the classic tale Little Red Riding Hood. Many movie versions have been made of this story. Regardless of the viewing audience, would you just grab any one of them to show at an event? I think not! Figure 86a shows just a few of the different versions that have very disparate approaches.

If you put *Little Dead Rotting Hood* up at your child's birthday party, you'd probably lose all of your future playdates! At a child's party, you'd better go with *Hoodwinked*. However, if you put *Little Dead Rotting Hood* up at a college party on Halloween night, it could be a big hit. The important thing is that different audiences want to hear the story in different ways. Regardless of which movie version you play, the audience will come away with the basic premise of the story even as the specifics of the delivery of the basic premise vary widely. What will succeed with one audience may fail miserably with another.

Movie Title	Director and Year	Format and Approach
Red Riding Hood	Randal Kleiser, 2006	Live Cast Movie
Hoodwinked	Cory and Todd Edwards, 2005	Modern Animated Comedy
Little Dead Rotting Hood	Jared Cohn, 2016	Horror Movie
Little Red Riding Hood	Toshiyuki Hiruma, Takashi, 1995	Classic Animated Tale

FIGURE 86A Same Story, Very Different Target Audiences!

It is no different when presenting data-driven content. A marketing team is going to care most about how a recommended action will lift marketing results and how it will be perceived by customers. A finance team is going to care most about the costs and ROI. The legal team is going to care most about ensuring that the company isn't exposed to legal risk. In the end, your overall story points and recommendations are the same for each audience. However, you will need to emphasize and order things differently to succeed with each group.

Gloss over the legal considerations with the marketing team and then drill into the projected lift. With the finance team, gloss over the lift, but then focus on the costs and ROI. Each audience will hear the full story, but they'll also have their specific preferences and viewpoints addressed in the delivery. Often, you can leave the presentation slides themselves mostly untouched while adjusting your verbal commentary and how long you focus on each slide. However, it is an absolute must to adjust your delivery for each audience.

In a situation with a broad and diverse audience, attempt to give everyone's needs a little bit of focus while acknowledging to the audience that additional conversations may be required for different stakeholders to drill into more of the details they care most about. People will understand that you can't be as precise in your targeting with a broad group. However, give a little more emphasis to the points most relevant to whichever audience member(s) you most need to influence.

Tip 87: Focus on Time, Not Slide Counts

One thing that drives me crazy is when people worry about how many slides you should have for a given time allotment. Not only is this not the right way to organize a presentation but also everyone has different opinions on the right number of "minutes per slide." I've heard one minute, two minutes, and even five minutes per slide used as a rule of thumb. Which is correct? Any of them can be . . . depending on the content.

Every slide is different. I have some slides that I talk through in 30 seconds or less. I have other slides that I talk through for 10 minutes or more. An audience won't notice how many slides you cover if they blend into the background of the flow of a compelling story and you finish on time.

The slide in Figure 87a can be covered very quickly. The slide in Figure 87b is the type of slide that might require minutes of discussion about each stage in the cycle as well as how they fit together.

When you add animations into the mix (see Tip 23), slide timing gets even murkier. Animations can turn a single slide into effectively many slides. I have seen people (including myself!) meet arbitrary slide limits by using complex animations to combine multiple slides into one.

Focus on creating a presentation that gets your points across succinctly, clearly, and with as few slides as possible. However, the slide count doesn't matter. What matters is that you complete your presentation in the time allotted while meeting the presentation's objectives. If your dry run (see Tip 83) shows you within the time limit, do not stress over having "too many" or "too few" slides. Just hit your time!

Our Project Team

The core project team was comprised of:

- Joe Winesalot

- Sheck Cho

- Jane Smith

- Mark Meewords

FIGURE 87A A Slide That Can Be Covered Quickly

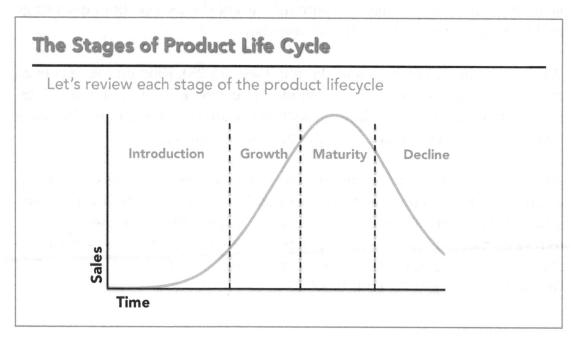

FIGURE 87B A Slide That Might Take a While to Cover

Tip 88: Always Be Prepared for a Short Presentation

Tip 8 probably made you hope that you are asked for a long presentation next time. If so, I have bad news. Even if you are asked for a long presentation, you must also be ready for a short presentation. "How can that be?!?!," you ask.

Even when there is no official question-and-answer slot, you can be sure that someone will ask questions. Next, you will almost always lose time as people come to the room and get settled. Between a few stragglers, some introductions, and a little small talk, you just lost more time. You may also be but one part of a broader agenda. When early speakers run long, those later in the agenda get squeezed on time. But none of these are the biggest time killers.

The higher up the chain your audience, the more likely that they will come late and/or leave early and/or be pulled out of the meeting temporarily in the middle. All of these will take from your time. In my career, I have had many occasions where an hour meeting turned into 15 or 20 minutes at the last minute. I once had a meeting with a chief marketing officer that went from a dedicated hour to 5 minutes walking together in the hall. Good thing I had my "elevator pitch" version ready!

All of that implies that if you aren't ready to make all of your key points quickly if necessary, you won't get to finish your story and you'll leave the audience hanging. It is very hard to be persuasive when you don't make all your arguments and don't get to your conclusions.

Always plan ahead by identifying what you would cut out first, second, and so on if you get crunched for time. That makes it easier to adjust at show-time. I think some of my best presentations have been those where I had to compress my content well below what I was comfortable with at the last minute. By preparing in advance to cut down the content, I was ready to do it, and the compressed time forced me to be highly focused and efficient with my delivery. Focused and efficient delivery is what audiences want regardless of the time you have. If you can pull off your presentation even when the audience knows they substantively cut your time, you'll score big points.

Tip 98 will discuss why you should always have multiple backup plans in case there are issues with technology. One of these backups is a printed version of your slides. I really like the PowerPoint feature that allows you to print four, six, or nine slides on a single page. This format lets you see what's coming next with just enough detail to remind you what you need to say. See Figure 88a.

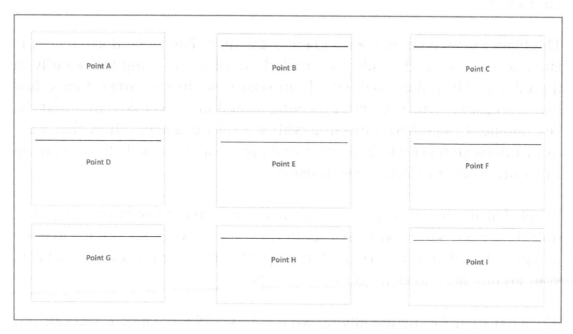

FIGURE 88A PowerPoint Printout of Multiple Slides

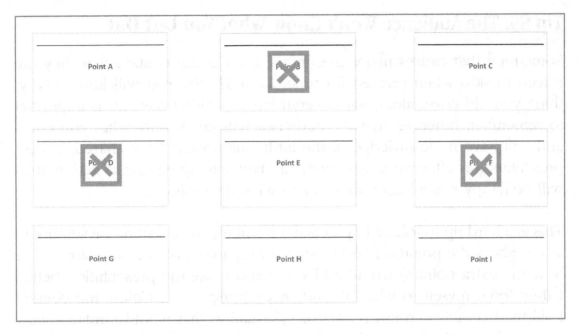

FIGURE 88B Mark Off Points to Skip

On that printout, mark which slides you'll skip if pressed for time and in what priority. If you lose time up-front, you can quickly hide the slides you need to skip. If you're delayed while presenting, just skip past the slides. I have had many occasions where I was looking down at my slide overviews at the front of the room and thinking, "That one has to go now. Uh oh, another question, I'll skip this one, too." I will mark out each slide with a pen as in Figure 88b. This trick has helped me keep my cool under pressure.

Tip 89: The Audience Won't Know What You Left Out

Something that causes many presenters angst is the content that they are forced to skip when pressed for time, as in Tip 88. You will know everything you did cover along with everything you didn't cover. It is important to remember, however, that the audience will know only what you cover and will have no knowledge of the additional material not shared. If your presentation is effective in getting the audience to agree to take action, they will be happy while being oblivious to what they missed.

This is a hard tip to follow in practice. I routinely must remind myself not to worry about the point(s) I had to skip. In my mind, of course, I stress over how the extra point(s) would add value and make the presentation better. I then force myself to take the audience's perspective. Unless the content I skipped contains critical pieces of information that would fundamentally change the audience's opinion of, and willingness to act on, my presentation, then the missed content has a negligible impact.

This tip can come into play as you prepare and not just when you are forced to shorten your presentation at the last minute. Often, I'll have a range of points I think are worthy of mention. Once I lay them all out, it becomes clear that I have more material than I can cover in the time that I have been allotted. In that situation, I must cut points during my preparation. As I struggle to decide what to cut, I focus on identifying the points that are either the least impactful or most redundant to other parts of my story. I can usually find a way to cut points so that I am still happy with my presentation and the reception I think it will receive. I accept the need to cut, I make the cuts, and I move on.

I moderate a lot of conference panels, and this tip also comes into play during those sessions. I always have a set of questions that I plan to ask the panelists. Inevitably, between people talking longer than expected and audience questions, I can't get to all the questions. Although I may be disappointed that I didn't get to ask a couple of my questions, I remind myself that the audience never knew the questions existed. If a panel runs smoothly, who cares about questions not asked?

To illustrate how this tip works in the context of this book, can you name one or two topics that were originally planned for the book but ended up being cut? Of course not!

Tip 90: Scale Figures to Be Relatable

The scale used to discuss findings can affect how easily the audience is able to comprehend the results. Nontechnical audiences have trouble processing small fractions or very large numbers. For example, nonprofits often make claims such as "For every semester we provide our free tutoring services to a student, their test scores rise by 10 points!" This approach is a great way to make impacts very tangible and relatable.

You must determine what scale will best enable the audience to appreciate your results. Consider the statement "For every dollar we invest in free tutoring, test scores rise by 0.01 points." Given that a dollar is a small amount of money, the impact of each dollar should be small. As a result, the claim doesn't sound remotely impressive. The fix? Change the scale! Instead say, "For every $1,000 invested in our free tutoring, test scores rise by 10 points." While maintaining the exact same mathematical relationship, it sounds much more impressive. It is also a fair scale to use because $1,000 is about what a semester of tutoring costs.

Similarly, analytical results are often put in context of odds. "For every shot of vodka consumed in a year, the chance of a drunken injury goes up by 0.1%" doesn't sound so bad. "For every gallon of vodka consumed over a year, the chance of a drunken injury goes up by 10%" sounds more concerning. Once again, the scale chosen affects how relatable the information is and how it is perceived.

Figure 90a makes a meaningful point with a bad choice of scale. It sounds meaningless. Figure 90b adjusts the scale and gets your attention.

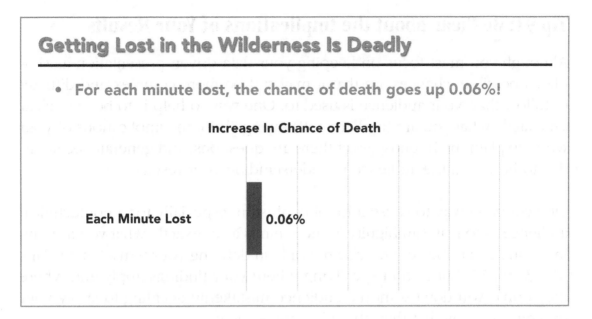

FIGURE 90A This Scale Is Hard to Relate To

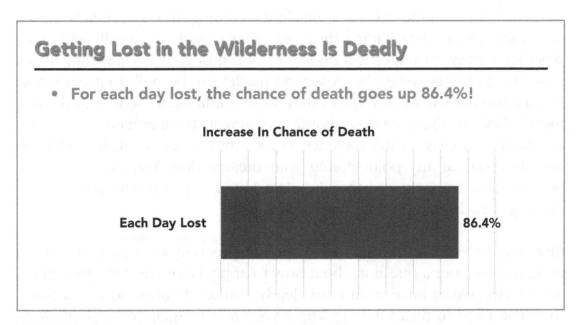

FIGURE 90B This Scale Is Very Easy to Relate To

Tip 91: Be Clear about the Implications of Your Results

Although you must focus on keeping your data-driven presentation as simple as possible, chances are that it may still be more complex and difficult to follow than your audience is used to. One way to help is to be very clear on exactly what you are (and are not!) saying about the implications of your work. Explain the bounds, ask if there are questions, and generally be attentive to how well the audience is understanding your results.

One common way to cause a lot of confusion, especially for a nontechnical audience, is to leave ambiguity in their minds as to exactly what you are saying. You need to be very precise not only in defining your terms (as per Tips 31, 33, 56, 57) but also in specifying where your findings apply and where they don't. You don't want the audience mistakenly deciding to apply your findings in a way that they shouldn't apply them.

Consider an example where a machine learning model predicts which customers will be late paying their bill. That model specifically says only whether a given customer will be late or not. It doesn't say anything about how late customers might be. A second model can be built to predict how late a customer will be, given that they were predicted to be late by the first model. Both of those models sound very similar to untrained ears, and it would be very easy for the audience to get confused as to which model you are discussing at any point during your presentation. You need to define both models precisely and then be clear about which model you are discussing at each point in time during your talk.

One way to validate that you have spoken precisely enough is to ask an audience member a question about how to apply what you have presented. If they struggle to answer and are clearly confused about how to answer, then you need to recap how to apply your results again to help the audience along. Your practice run with a confidant (see Tip 84) is also a great time to check this.

As you prepare your slides and your story, think about how you'll precisely explain each piece of data and each implication from the start. The more you plan and practice to ensure that what you present will be precise and clear (see Tip 83), the more likely you are to have your presentation viewed that way by your audience.

Tip 92: Call Out Any Ethical Concerns

Due to data breaches, faked research results, invasive use of personal data, and more, people across the globe have become much more sensitive to ethics and privacy. You are taking a big risk if you don't proactively think through potential ethical concerns related to any scientific or analytical work you undertake. You then have a responsibility to inform your audience of any concerns.

In my world of analytics and data science, the need for consideration of ethics permeates all stages of the conception, creation, and deployment of a new analytical process. Figure 92a shows a generic, yet typical, process. How do ethical considerations enter every phase?

1. Define problem and analysis plan.
   - Is what you are trying to do ethical? For example, predicting which employees will experience mental illness with the intent to fire them is not.
2. Acquire and prepare data.
   - Is it ethical to use the data you plan to use for the purpose you plan to use it? For example, should medical records be linked with credit records?
3. Perform analysis.
   - Are the completed models biased against certain groups?
4. Deploy process for use.
   - Are there controls to ensure the model is only used as intended?
5. Monitor and maintain process.
   - Are there protocols to ensure the model works as intended?

There are so many ethical considerations that I released a book titled *97 Things about Ethics Everyone in Data Science Should Know* (O'Reilly Media, 2020) focused solely on the subject. At a minimum, commit to being intentional about considering ethics in any of the technical work that you do. Calling out ethical concerns isn't just the right thing to do, but it is increasingly necessary to protect your reputation and that of your organization.

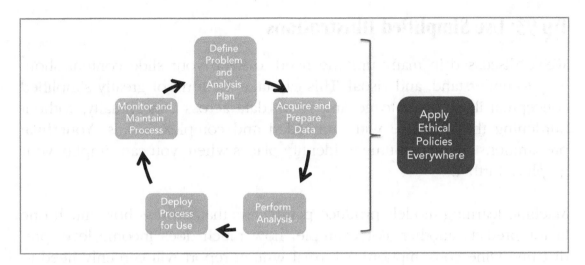

FIGURE 92A Where Does Ethics Need Consideration?

Tip 93: Use Simplified Illustrations

We've discussed in many tips the need to keep your slide content short, easy to understand, and visual. This can take the form of greatly simplified conceptual illustrations to get important data across conceptually, without burdening the audience with unneeded and complex details. Your final preparations are a great time to identify places where you can simplify your graphics further.

Machine learning models produce parameters that express how much one factor predicts another. For example, how much does income level predict fine wine consumption? A formal written report will certainly need to contain details about the parameter values, model diagnostics, and more. However, do you really need to show your live audience all that detail? No! Comparing complicated numbers in their heads isn't something you want the audience doing when they are supposed to be listening to you.

In the case of relative measures such as parameter estimates, one option is to focus on the direction and relative magnitude/importance of each parameter with a graphical icon, such as an arrow or a speedometer, instead of a raw number. This enables the audience to quickly see what's positive and what's negative. If they are really interested in the parameter values, they can ask and you can jump to the appendix that has the numbers. (Of course you will have this in an appendix per Tip 19, won't you?) This approach streamlines your discussion and increases audience comprehension.

Figure 93a shows a table of parameters as values, which is the typical approach. A nontechnical audience may not be sure what to do with these. Figure 93b uses arrows to express the information more visually. It enables the audience to grasp the core information, but with limited mental effort.

Factors Effecting Fine Wine Consumption

- Age and income have the largest impact

Model Parameters

Factor	Parameter Estimate
Age	5.2
Education Level	1.3
Income	9.7
Cigarette Smoking	-1.4
# Nearby Wine Stores	0.2

FIGURE 93A Typical Approach with Exact Figures

Factors Effecting Fine Wine Consumption

- Age and income have the largest impact

Relative Impacts

Factor	Relative Impact
Age	⬆
Education Level	⬌
Income	⬆
Cigarette Smoking	⬇
# Nearby Wine Stores	⬌

FIGURE 93B Simplified Approach Emphasizing General Direction

Tip 94: Don't Include Low-Value Information

This is another tip that should be really obvious, but apparently it isn't to a lot of presenters because this error occurs frequently! Few would question that including low-value information is pointless, so don't be the person who includes it. However, "valuable" depends on context and perspective. As you finalize preparations, keep an eye out for places where information you've included isn't as valuable as you hoped when you compiled it.

Consider an experiment testing if some sensor brands have more defects than others. From a technical perspective, it may seem worthwhile to include detailed data showing a negligible difference in defect rates across multiple sensors. Figure 94a shows a table with nearly identical data that adds little value and will distract the audience from your story. Don't make the audience look at a table with 10 nearly identical numbers to validate for themselves that they are almost identical.

From a typical audience's perspective, they have no interest in seeing such data while you present. They would prefer to take your word for it if you just stated that there was no difference and moved on. If the data shows that every brand has within rounding error of the same defect rate, then call out that fact and display the rate that the sensors cluster tightly around. Figure 94b calls out that the numbers were similar and shows the average, minimum, and maximum. There are many fewer numbers to interpret, and the point can be seen immediately. Of course, you can have the detailed data ready in an appendix in case someone did care.

Valuable differences aren't always large differences, however. Sometimes even very small differences matter. This tip is about value in terms of importance, not magnitude.

Sensor Test Summary

- All sensors broke at effectively the same rate, with none having defect rates more than 1/10th percent different

Sensor	Defect Rate	Sensor	Defect Rate
Brand 1	10.15%	Brand 6	10.14%
Brand 2	10.12%	Brand 7	10.11%
Brand 3	10.17%	Brand 8	10.17%
Brand 4	10.11%	Brand 9	10.16%
Brand 5	10.19%	Brand 10	10.13%

FIGURE 94A There Is Little Value in Seeing All the Specific Defect Rates

Sensor Test Summary

- All sensors broke at effectively the same rate, with none having defect rates more than 1/10th percent different

Average Sensor Defect Rate	10.15%
Minimum	10.11%
Maximum	10.19%

FIGURE 94B A More Focused Way to Make the Point

Tip 95: Make Critical Numbers Stand Out

Some pieces of information are far more important to the audience than others. As you finalize your preparations, make the most important pieces of information very easy for the audience to focus on. In Tip 23, we discussed highlighting information using animations to control the flow of information. In this tip, we address it from the perspective of drawing your audience's attention to important information. When making your final preparations, as you identify numbers that are especially critical, make them stand out.

There are multiple ways to highlight numbers in a table or chart. You can circle them, draw an arrow pointing to them, make them a different color, make them a different font size, bold them, or any combination of those techniques. You can do this with or without the animations discussed in Tip 23. The goal is to make it very easy for the audience to see the most critical pieces of information you will be discussing.

Don't underestimate the power and impact of this technique. When tables and charts are displayed, everyone in the audience will immediately attempt to interpret what they see and determine what is important. This takes mental energy, takes their attention from you, and risks them focusing on something you didn't intend.

When critical pieces of information are highlighted, people's attention will go straight there because they will assume that is where their attention should be. Combined with your narrative discussing the same information, it will keep the audience on track for hearing and comprehending your message. Figure 95a shows a basic table with nothing highlighted. Figure 95b demonstrates several different ways that the critical number can be highlighted for the audience.

The Path to an "A" in Bill's Class Is Clear

Student Segment	Percent with an "A"
Honor Roll Students	83.2%
Frequently Sleep in Class	29.5%
Skipped Class Regularly	15.3%
Brought Bill Gifts	99.9%

FIGURE 95A It Isn't Clear where the Audience Should Focus

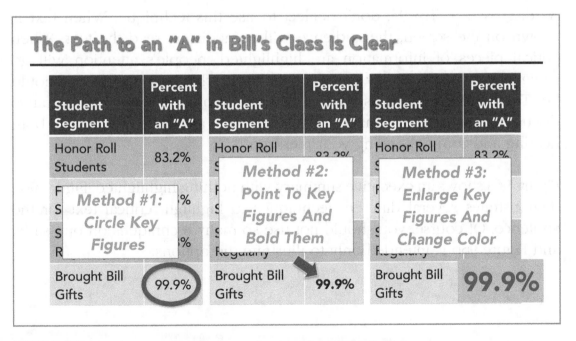

FIGURE 95B Options to Draw Attention to the Main Point

Tip 96: Make Important Text Stand Out Too

Tip 95 discussed drawing audience attention to critical numbers within tables or graphs. Another good practice is to draw audience attention to important text on your slides. As with highlighting numbers, highlighting text helps focus the audience on the most important parts of your content, which will often be some statement of impact, value, or risk. As you make your final preparations, look for opportunities to focus your audience on the critical text.

There are many ways to highlight important text. You can bold the text, make it a different color, italicize it, underline it, or any combination of those techniques. Regardless of the technique, the goal is to make it easy for the audience to identify the most critical pieces of information that you will be discussing. By now, you know to keep text to a minimum and so you'll be highlighting just a couple words out of a short sentence.

As discussed in Tip 95, don't neglect to use this technique. When text is shown on the screen, the audience will immediately read the text. When critical pieces of information are highlighted, people's attention will go straight there because they will assume that is where their attention should be. This is true for text as well as figures. Combined with your narrative discussing the same information, it will keep the audience on track for both hearing and comprehending your message.

Figure 96a shows an executive summary with nothing highlighted. Figure 96b demonstrates several different techniques to highlight critical text for the audience. Of course, you should not use so many techniques on one slide, and Figure 96b is intended only to illustrate the options.

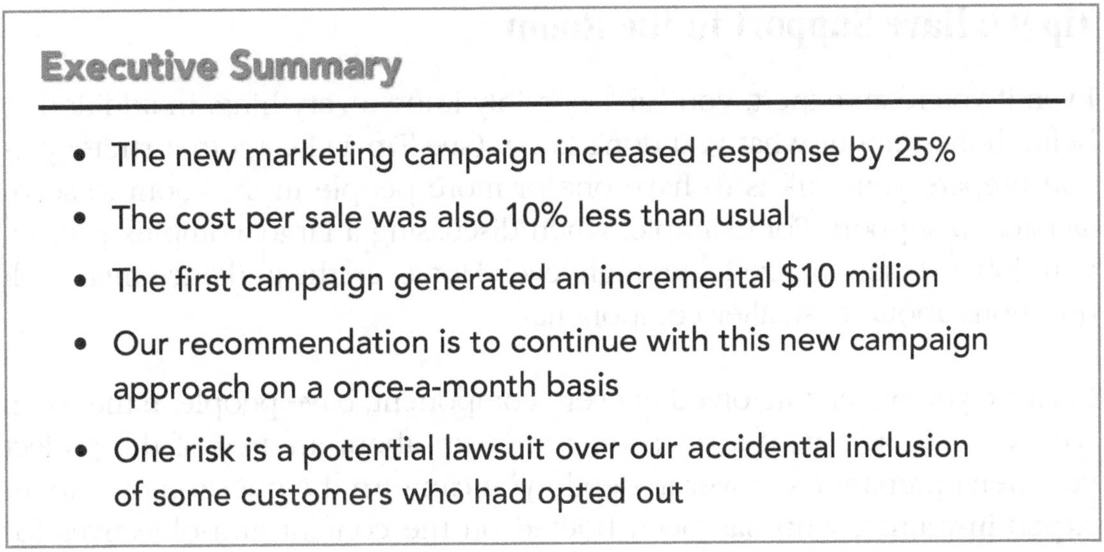

Executive Summary

- The new marketing campaign increased response by 25%

- The cost per sale was also 10% less than usual

- The first campaign generated an incremental $10 million

- Our recommendation is to continue with this new campaign approach on a once-a-month basis

- One risk is a potential lawsuit over our accidental inclusion of some customers who had opted out

FIGURE 96A It Isn't Clear where the Audience Should Focus

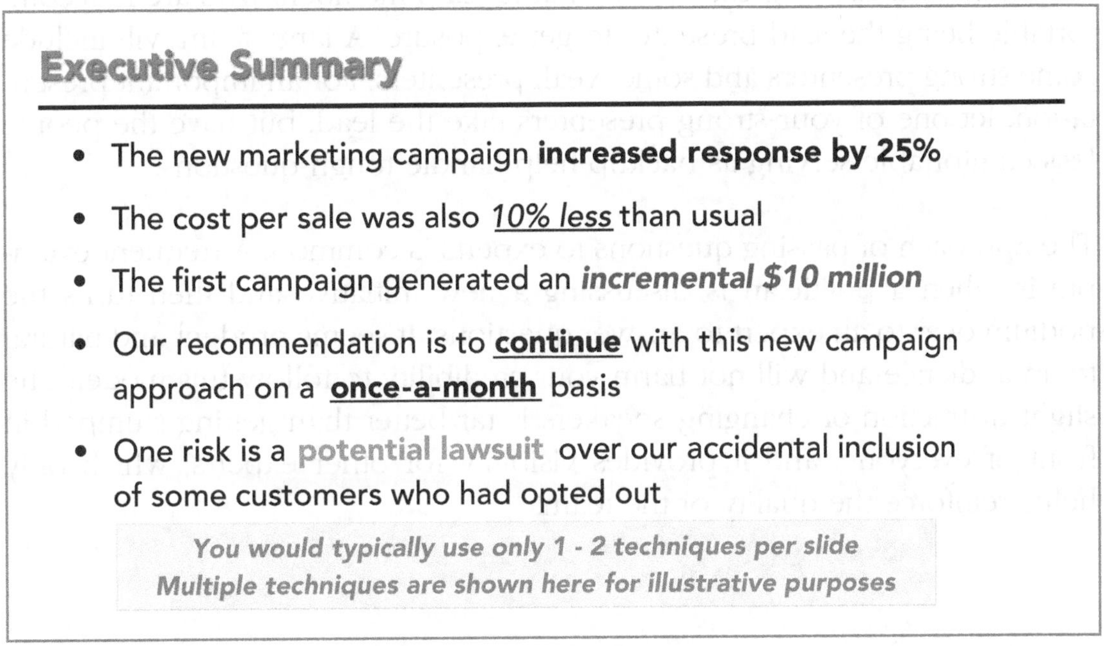

Executive Summary

- The new marketing campaign **increased response by 25%**

- The cost per sale was also _10% less_ than usual

- The first campaign generated an _incremental $10 million_

- Our recommendation is to **continue** with this new campaign approach on a **once-a-month** basis

- One risk is a potential lawsuit over our accidental inclusion of some customers who had opted out

> *You would typically use only 1 - 2 techniques per slide*
> *Multiple techniques are shown here for illustrative purposes*

FIGURE 96B Options to Draw Attention to the Main Points

Tip 97: Have Support in the Room

Even if you're an expert, you can't possibly know everything. In addition to being honest about what you don't know (see Tip 111), another strategy as you prepare your talk is to have one or more people in the room to serve as backup support. For example, when discussing a large, complex project, your job is to summarize it at a high level. However, the audience might ask questions about its smaller components.

Because you weren't involved in every component, have people in the room who were. That way, if a question comes up about an area of the project you aren't prepared to cover in depth, you can turn the question over to an expert-in-waiting who has been briefed on the content and objectives for the meeting. This also helps demonstrate the depth of your team.

This strategy is also a great way to enable team members who are less comfortable being the lead presenter to get exposure. A large team will include some strong presenters and some weak presenters. For an important presentation, let one of your strong presenters take the lead, but have the people less comfortable serving as backup help handle tough questions.

The approach of passing questions to experts is common. A frequent example is when a politician is discussing a new initiative and then turns the podium over to an expert to answer questions. It seems prudent and natural to an audience and will not harm your credibility to follow this model. The slight distraction of changing speakers is far better than getting stumped in front of everyone, and it provides visibility for other experts, which only helps reinforce the quality of the team!

Tip 98: Always Have Several Backup Plans

When you're finalizing preparation for the big presentation, never underestimate the number of things that can go wrong! If you assume that your computer, the projector, and the audio system will work as expected, then you risk having a disaster presentation. Over the years, I have had many permutations of problems.

Once, a coworker and I were co-presenting at a conference. She put our slides up as we started. Right as my turn to talk started, her battery died! (Don't ask me why she didn't plug in.) By the time she found her power cord, rebooted the machine, and got it connected to the projector, my 20-minute section was complete. Luckily, I had my slide thumbnails printed (see Tips 9 and 88). I stood on the stage and said everything I had planned to say, but without the slides being projected. Ideal? No. Did it work well enough? Yes.

At another conference, I confirmed with the show's tech lead that my presentation was loaded and ready to go. He even showed me where the file was in a folder, but I didn't open it at that time. As a result, I left my computer bag in my car's trunk. Of course, when I went to present, I found that the local file was corrupted and wouldn't open. I had to run down to the car and get my computer and started 15 minutes late as a result. That is the last time I ever left any of my backup items anywhere but with me!

There are many forms of and methods for backup:

- Get to the room early to set up and deal with any issues that arise.
- Connect with the room's tech team well ahead of your session to validate that all technologies and files are as expected.
- Have a printout of your full slides and/or slide thumbnails (see Tips 9 and 88).
- Have your presentation on a USB drive.

- Have your own slide clicker because room clickers frequently don't work (see Tip 99).
- Have your presentation in an email you can forward to another computer from your phone.
- Have every type of video connection cable your computer supports, plus adapters for other types of connections that your computer doesn't support.

Even with all of those in place, something else might still go wrong (I once had a fire alarm cost me 40 of my 60 minutes as we evacuated the building). But, at least you'll be prepared for the most common problems.

Tip 99: Use a Slide Clicker

I always have my personal slide clicker in my bag. My current one only cost about $15. It is shaped like a pen and fits in my hand so that the audience can barely tell that I have it. It has a standard USB plug-in that connects to the clicker wirelessly, so it works on virtually any computer.

A clicker gives you full control of your slides from wherever you are standing. It also avoids forcing you to return to the computer every time you want to advance a slide. In a small room, tapping the keyboard works okay because there isn't much room for you to move anyway. In most presentations, it will be a distraction. Per Tip 106, you should move around during your presentation, and needing to return to home base for every slide change will limit your ability to do so.

You should avoid having someone advance the slides for you. It is rare that a slide changer knows exactly what you'll say and when to click to advance slides seamlessly. In 99% of the presentations I've seen with an official slide changer, the speaker has to say "next slide" each time, which is distracting. Things only get worse when you need to go back a few slides and you must say "another one, another one, oops too far" until you find it. With your clicker, you can just go to the right slide.

If you use action settings (see Tip 24), then you'll need a fancier clicker with mouse functionality or you'll be forced to return to home base to make use of an action. However, actions are typically at a break point in the flow and so this isn't as distracting as usual.

Tip 100: Do Not Send Your Presentation in Advance

It is not unusual when you are preparing a presentation to be asked for a copy in advance. I know many speakers who proactively send their presentations in advance to the audience, whether requested to or not. I strongly recommend against sending anything in advance unless you are given no choice.

For example, if the executive team you are presenting to requires everyone to send slides in advance with no exception, then you are stuck. Outside of a firm mandate, offer to send out a copy as soon as the presentation is over so that any last-minute changes will be accounted for. I typically just ignore a request for advance slides and far more often than not, the person asking forgets until I show up to the presentation. At that point, I commit to sending as soon as the meeting is over.

Why is it bad to send the slides in advance? There are several reasons:

- You want the audience to hear your story directly from you. When you send your slides in advance, they'll have already seen your punchlines, but without your narrative and context. Like knowing the punchline to a joke before it is told, the big "aha" moments you discuss won't seem so big if the audience already knows them.
- Many in the audience won't read your slides prior to the meeting but will instead spend much of the start of the meeting looking through them and ignoring you. This still has all the negatives of the prior point with the added downside of loss of attention during the presentation.
- After reading your slides, people will form opinions, draw conclusions, and even start making plans on the partial information they extract from your slides. You will now have to change their minds, which is hard to do.
- You might make last-minute changes. It hurts your credibility and your flow to have to say, "This slide was updated and won't match what you have in front of you."

In cases when I have been forced to send slides in advance, I start my presentation by asking people not to read through them as I talk. I explain that I'll be providing important context for the facts in the slides and that they'll get the most from the session if they consider the handout to be notes for later.

Another common situation is when an administrative assistant or technical support person asks for your slides to load them on a meeting room computer for projecting. In these cases, I'll first ask if I can just connect my computer instead. They usually say that I can and are relieved not to have to worry about anything on their end. If someone is adamant about using the equipment in the room (many conferences are), I supply the slides but ask that they only be placed on the machine in the room and not distributed beforehand. I also make clear that the raw PowerPoint version should never be shared with anyone and should be deleted from the computer when I am done. Almost everyone will comply with those requests.

Last, whenever you do share your content, be sure to include copyright and confidentiality notices at the bottom. Also, always share your content as a PDF so that nobody can edit it, whether accidentally or not, and then pass on a changed version. Make sure that only your story is shared and only as you wrote it!

Delivering: Giving the Presentation

When the big day has arrived and you're stepping to the front of the room, there are still a range of things to focus on if you want your presentation to be a success. This section will cover various presentation mechanics to use, as well as some important principles to follow, as you deliver your data-driven presentation. Here are some of the concepts discussed in this section:

- Read the room and adapt your delivery to what you see.
- Handle difficult audience members.
- Be honest and confident while not hedging too much.
- Drive home the impacts of your work and related recommendations for action.
- Close with a "wow" to finish strong by tying the results to a larger context.

After all the work that went into getting ready for the big day, your final delivery will have a huge impact on whether those efforts pay off. Ensuring that you follow the guidance in this section will help you make your delivery compelling. If you win the trust and confidence of the audience, you can motivate them to embrace your conclusions and act on your recommendations. This, in turn, will allow your efforts to be a resounding success!

Tip 101: Do Not Read Your Slides . . . Ever!

One of the single most destructive things you can do to ruin any live presentation is to read from your slides. We have all been in a meeting where someone puts up slides, turns to the screen instead of the audience, and then proceeds to read the slide word for word. There are many reasons that is a bad thing to do and it is so obviously bad that it seems silly to be including this tip. However, given that people routinely read their slides, the tip is necessary.

For starters, reading from the screen adds no value. People can read the screen on their own. If all you want the audience to do is learn exactly what is written on the slide, simply put up the slide and tell them to read it. Then, sit down and stay out of the way. However, there is no point to scheduling a presentation in that case. Instead, save the audience's time and just send them the slides to read on their own and offer to answer questions via email.

When a presenter is reading their slides, they must completely ignore the audience and either face the screen or stare down at their notes. That is not engaging for the audience, and it leads to a monotone delivery that makes the experience painful. Remember the horrible teacher from the movie *Ferris Bueller's Day Off*? Anyone? Anyone? Who wants to sound like him? Anyone? Anyone?

The best way to avoid the urge to read from your slides is to remember some of the other tips in the book such as keeping text to a minimum (Tip 30); telling a story, not writing one (Tip 3); and keeping your slides visual and to the point (Tip 6). If your slides are done properly, the audience won't be able to get the full scope of your point from the slide. They will see that you have something valuable to communicate, but it is impossible to simply read the slide to successfully grasp it all. The audience will need and want to listen to your verbal narrative for the full context. This will be more engaging for the audience and will also force you to be better prepared and exude more energy.

Sometimes people read slides because they do not know their material well enough to do otherwise. Reading the slides is the wrong solution for that underlying problem. If you are so uncomfortable with your material that you feel you must read it, then you should not give the presentation. It will be a failure, guaranteed! Either postpone the presentation until you are ready or send out a written document instead.

The only time to make an exception to this rule is if there is a particularly important phrase, title, or name that must be repeated exactly. If, in the middle of several minutes of good commentary, you need to turn and read a direct quote, a specific policy point, or a specific name from the screen, that is okay if it seems natural in context. People won't mind a short line being read if they are enjoying your talk and they'll appreciate that you wanted the quote or statement to be accurate.

Tip 102: Read the Room and Adapt

You must become skilled at reading the mood and reactions of your audience and adapting your presentation on the fly. No matter how well you plan and prepare your data-driven presentation, it is impossible to predict how your audience will react until you are presenting. Technical people are not always the best at reading a room, so this skill may require intentional cultivation and practice if you come from a technical background.

In an ideal scenario, you know what your audience hopes to hear, it lines up perfectly with your findings and narrative, and there are no political undertones that might cause resistance. In the real world that will rarely be true, and any number of things can cause an audience to develop a challenging, defensive, or even outright hostile attitude.

If you present right after some very bad news was announced, your audience will start in a negative mindset. Sometimes, partial (or even false) information gets disseminated in advance about your presentation, which can cause audience members to start on the defensive. If you have misunderstood what the audience is hoping for, it can lead to immediate pushback. These are a few of many reasons why an audience might be difficult from the start.

Even if your audience is in a positive mindset at the outset, that can change. One of your findings might be more controversial than you expected. Someone might have a higher personal stake in the status quo than you realized. Your presentation might have errors or poorly worded phrasing (but not if you have followed the tips in this book!), which leads the audience to lose confidence in you and your results. Whatever the reason, an audience that starts friendly will not always stay that way.

If you sense the room turning against you, you need to identify why that is and try to mitigate it as soon as possible. You can even ask, "Some of you look concerned or unconvinced. Can you help me understand why that is?" Then, based on what you hear, you need to shift focus to addressing the concern(s) raised. There is no guarantee that you will swing the audience back your way. However, if the audience can see that you are attempting to address the concerns raised, they will be more forgiving.

In an extreme case, a major issue arises that must be resolved before the audience will be able to support your findings. If so, end your presentation and suggest that it be continued after the issue is resolved. This way, you stop the bleeding and prevent any further points you plan to make from being associated with what is, for now, an unsuccessful presentation.

Thus far, we have focused on an audience turning negative. You must also identify when an audience has been won over and does not need any more convincing. An old saying goes, "Know when to stop selling!" If an audience is totally on board and ready to act, then consider skipping or greatly shortening the remainder of your presentation. Don't risk derailing the excitement. More data and information can help win a skeptical mind over. More data and information, if not needed, can also accidentally place doubt in the mind of someone who is already won over. Don't sell past "yes"!

Tip 103: Do Not Look at the Screen!

I can't imagine anyone arguing the against the merit of a presenter making eye contact with the audience instead of turning around to look at the screen. Unfortunately, this is one of the most common errors made. Although less-experienced presenters look at the screen all the time, even experienced presenters fall into this trap. Looking at the screen while you talk totally disengages you from your audience. If there are times that you need to take a quick glance to refresh yourself on a number, you can get away with it if you do it quickly and rarely. Maintaining eye contact with the audience should be your primary goal. One exception is when, as we discuss in Tip 104, you want to make a show of physically pointing to something particularly important on the screen.

People usually look at the screen because they are not comfortable with their material and they are using the slides as cheat sheets. Remember that in Tips 9 and 88, we talked about having a printout in front of you. Although it also isn't ideal to stare down at your notes, at least you are facing the audience. Large conferences have "confidence monitors" by the stage. These are screens facing the speaker instead of the audience. I love when I give a keynote and they have these because if I do need a quick peek at my slide, it is a simple glance down instead of a full turn around with my head looking up.

You can mimic a confidence monitor by having the computer that is projecting positioned such that you can see its screen. If I am presenting in a long conference room, for example, I'll put my laptop in the middle of the table at the end I will be presenting from so that it is facing me. It doesn't distract anyone in the audience, but it lets me see what's on the screen without looking behind me. If I am in a large room with a lot of individual tables, I'll put my laptop on the table closest to the front of the room by where I will be speaking.

In a worst-case scenario, you may be asked to present from a computer tied into a room's system and it may be positioned in a way that you can't see it. In that case you have two options. First, you can place the slide overview printouts discussed in Tips 9 and 88 on the table or podium in front of you. Another option is to still put your computer where you want it and then advance the slides on your computer and the room's computer at the same time using two clickers. This can be tricky, but it can work.

Tip 104: Physically Point to Important Information

During a live presentation, it can add some flair to your talk to walk over to the screen and point to something important or to point a laser pointer at a key element of your slide. We talked in Tip 103 about never looking at the screen. As with any rule, there are exceptions.

One of the exceptions to Tip 103 is when you are making a critical point while highlighting information through your actions in front of the room. To highlight an especially critical number or statement, pause your talking, walk to the screen, point to the item you want to highlight, and then turn back to the audience to describe why it is so important. This approach should be used sparingly so that it doesn't become overdone.

When presenting online, you can't physically highlight points. Although some online meeting systems have a "pointer" that you can use, it isn't as impactful as in real life and I have rarely seen it used effectively. So, what do you do online in the place of physically pointing to something?

You'll read in various tips in this book about the effective use of slide animations and highlighted content. Those techniques are the key to meeting your needs online. When there is an important number you want to draw attention to in an online or hybrid environment, consider one of the methods from Tips 23, 95, and 96 to do it. Although those methods will enable you to make your point online, they are also great approaches when presenting in person. Even if you plan to walk and point to a number for effect, it doesn't hurt to have it highlighted on the screen as well.

Tip 105: Don't Let Bright Lights Throw You Off

When presenting in a conference room, classroom, or training facility, there is typically no special lighting. When presenting at a conference or major corporate event, especially if you are on the main stage, the environment will be very different. Main stages usually use professional lighting. In cases where the sessions are being filmed, this lighting is very, very bright, and it is often necessary to continually resist the urge to squint.

All those bright lights affect what you can see. Instead of seeing all the smiling faces in the audience, you are effectively blinded even as the audience sees you perfectly. This means that you may be able to make out general shapes of people, but you won't be able to see faces and reactions. This takes some getting used to.

The most common speaker reactions to the bright lights are to either look down to avoid the lights or to just look generally into space. Both of those approaches will look bad to your audience. You need to force yourself to look around and pretend as though you are making eye contact with the audience as you would usually do. Although you won't actually be making eye contact on your end, the people sitting near where you look will feel like you are looking at them. In their minds you *are* making eye contact.

When someone stares straight at their camera in an online meeting, as we'll discuss in Tip 107, your brain perceives that they are looking right at you. When you're looking around the room from a bright stage, you're using a similar perceptual trick to give your audience the impression that you are looking at them.

Tip 106: Don't Stand Still

You should not stand still during a live presentation. No matter how nervous you are, you must force yourself to project confidence. Movement is one way to do that. An early sign for me that a presentation is going to be boring is when the presenter stands directly behind a podium and doesn't move for the first few minutes. At that point, I freshen my caffeinated beverage!

It is very, very hard to be energetic and enthusiastic while standing still. The audience will also struggle to see your body language if you are hidden by a podium. By walking around with purpose, you inject energy into your story and keep the audience alert. This is because people's brains will take notice of motion and track it. As you move around, you can also make eye contact with people in different parts of the room and even move toward specific individuals to engage them. Depending on the projector configuration, you might be able to walk freely anywhere. In cases where you will substantively block the projector in some areas, move through those areas quickly to get to either side.

Getting comfortable with movement is another activity that you should consider filming yourself doing (see Tip 83). If you move too fast and too often, it can be distracting. If you stand still for long periods in between small bursts of movement, you will need to focus on moving more. You should also validate that you are standing straight and keeping your hands engaged, but not too active. If you do it right, the audience won't explicitly notice that you're moving around. They'll just notice that you are giving an engaging presentation. A final benefit of movement is that it helps keep you energized just like any physical activity does. Your own energy will drop if you remain perfectly still.

There are a few exceptions to this rule: (1) when you are forced to present in a very small room where there is simply no room to move; (2) when you are being filmed with a camera that cannot move, whether to support a hybrid online/in-person presentation or a video for later use, which will require you to be mostly stationary to stay in the frame; and (3) when there is only a single, stationary microphone on the podium. In such cases, unless the room is very large, I will turn off the mic and just talk extra loudly as I move. If the room is too large or you have a quiet voice, however, you could be stuck. Luckily, many large rooms are equipped with wireless microphones that will solve the problem.

Of course, most of this tip ties to a live presentation in a room. If you are presenting in an online setting, then you'll unfortunately need to sit still in your seat in front of the camera like everyone else. This is one of the drawbacks to online presentations. Seeing just a face with a slide isn't nearly as compelling as seeing somebody live. Per the prior paragraph, hybrid sessions are also suboptimal because you'll be stuck staying within the camera's range for the remote audience. At least you'll not be just a face to the local, live audience in a hybrid setting.

Tip 107: When Presenting Online, Look Right at the Camera

When you look down at the images of audience members during an online presentation, your eyes are specifically *not* looking at your camera. This means that although you feel like you're doing the right thing by looking at another person as you would do in real life, the audience sees you looking down and away from them. You are, in fact, disconnecting rather than connecting with your audience.

Whether you are doing a formal presentation or just having a chat, force yourself to look squarely at your camera and ignore the video thumbnails of other participants on your screen. You may be wondering what the point of a video call is if you shouldn't look at the video of the other participants. I wonder the same thing all the time!

It takes a lot of practice to look consistently at your camera because it feels unnatural. I still find my eyes drifting, especially if someone is asking me a question because the natural reaction is to look at them. I am in the habit of validating where my eyes are looking regularly during an online presentation. This same technique is used on television. Notice that on news shows, guests and hosts often aren't looking at each other, but at a camera as they talk. Similarly, you should talk to the camera and not thumbnail images of your audience.

Figure 107a shows me looking directly at the camera. Notice how it seems I am looking right at you. Figure 107b shows me looking at my shared slide in the middle of the screen. It makes me seem disconnected. Figure 107c shows me looking at the bottom corner of my screen, at someone's thumbnail. This looks even worse.

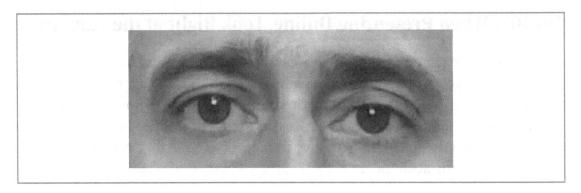

FIGURE 107A Looking at the Camera

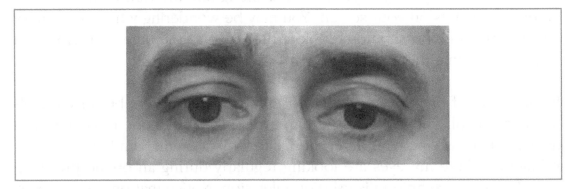

FIGURE 107B Looking Just below the Camera at a Slide

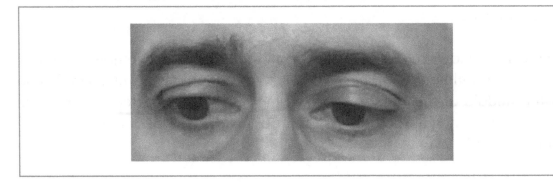

FIGURE 107C Looking at a Participant in the Bottom Corner

Tip 108: Anticipate Random and Irrelevant Questions

There will sometimes be people in your audience who simply don't understand what you are talking about and/or care about nothing except their own agenda. When such people are in your audience, you can get questions that seem random, irrelevant, or off track.

The way to react when getting such questions is to keep your composure. First, don't show that you are puzzled by the fact the question would be asked. Other audience members may be groaning inside (or even openly!) along with you, but you shouldn't react as the presenter. Also remember that a person with an agenda putting you in an awkward spot is usually just a side effect of their pursuit of their own needs. Try not to take it personally.

You can't just ignore an irrelevant question. You must find a way to graciously move past it. If the question is quick and easy to answer, give the answer and move on regardless of its relevance. If the question would take you off on a distracting and time-consuming tangent, explain that a proper answer will take more time than is available and offer to take the discussion offline. Others in the room will appreciate not having to sit through an off-topic discussion, and the person asking knows that you are willing to discuss it, albeit later. Everyone is happy!

In rare cases of someone who just won't let their question go, hope that others in the audience will step in to support tabling the question. A last resort is to call a short break and take the person aside to ask them respectfully to let the question be tabled. If that fails, you may be forced to take the tangent, however reluctantly.

Tip 109: Handle Difficult People with Grace

Tip 108 discusses being prepared for audience members who disrupt your presentation somewhat unintentionally. But what about someone who is unexpectedly adversarial, argumentative, and contentious after your presentation starts? Such an audience member can be more difficult to deal with. There are times someone disagrees with the entire premise of the results you are presenting, and they don't mean to be personal. They may have been against the project since your sponsor first discussed doing it. There are other times where someone is very clearly attacking you on a personal level. For the most part, you need to deal with both types of people in the same way.

First, recognize that most people do not like to see others disrupt a presentation, especially with open attacks. You probably have a lot of supporters in the audience who are unhappy with the attack, too, even if they don't speak up. Because you shouldn't show frustration or anger as the speaker, you will have to handle your adversary with grace and placate them enough to let you move on.

Unfortunately, there are cases where you have been given bad information or you truly made a mistake. In such situations, it can be understandable that an audience member is upset and combative, especially if they are affected. I was once given incorrect information by a client on how to interpret a data field. Based on that incorrect guidance, I found some unsettling trends that caused the VP over the affected area to get quite upset during my presentation. After I explained how we got the numbers, he was able to point out that a key premise was false. All I could do was apologize and offer to revisit the analysis with the now-correct information before moving on to the next part of the findings. If your attacker has a good point, as did that VP, acknowledge it, apologize, and move on.

Assuming your results are bulletproof, and someone is still being combative, then you need to try and handle them quickly and diplomatically. Perhaps you can answer their first question or even the first two, but you shouldn't devolve your presentation into a contentious one-on-one argument. Once it is clear the person is going to keep the attacks coming, suggest that the two of you take it offline and that you move on to the next point. As often as not, the person being difficult is frequently difficult in other situations as well. As a result, you'll have a lot of supporters in the room ready to back up your request to take it offline. When I have ended up in this uncomfortable situation, it is often other audience members who get the difficult person to stand down. Others know when attacks are unfair and unproductive and will often lend assistance.

In a rare case where nobody backs you up, you'll be faced with the no-win choice of either continuing the contentious debate or moving on over the highly vocal protests of your adversary. Choose the option to move on, commit to it, and push forward as best you can.

Tip 110: Don't Correct People in Front of the Room

Unless someone has totally misunderstood what you've said in a way that could lead to huge problems and thus requires immediate correction, then don't correct people in front of the room. You can always privately grab someone later to explain where they went wrong. Publicly correcting someone can have multiple negative impacts on the effectiveness of your data-driven presentation:

- It can embarrass or anger the person you correct (especially an executive in front of employees).
- It can scare other people from expressing their opinion for fear of being corrected.
- It can make you seem petty or overzealous when your clarification is hard for people to grasp.
- Depending on your delivery it can make you sound condescending and/ or arrogant.

None of those are something you want associated with you or your data-driven presentation. If you're unsure if something is important enough to warrant an explicit correction, then mention that there are some nuances worth discussing offline, but that for now it is best to move on. That lets you flag the need for clarification in a much less confrontational fashion.

In fact, you can often "correct" the person by saying that you can tell that you weren't effective in communicating your point based on the question or comment. Then, offer a more detailed explanation in hopes that it will address the concern. Another advantage of this approach is that if one person misunderstood something, it is likely others may have as well. So you can address what could be a bigger issue diplomatically by placing the blame for the misunderstanding on yourself.

The truth is that most times audience members misunderstand something, it is harmless. I wrote a blog (*The Benefits of Ignoring When Executives Misunderstand Artificial Intelligence,* International Institute For Analytics, January 2019) about how executives often misunderstand artificial intelligence (AI) in terms of how it works and where it may apply. I've had discussions with countless executives excited to "solve this problem using AI." My view is that if the executive is excited to have you solve their problem, then go with it! There is no upside to correcting them. Just accept the challenge to solve their problem, with or without AI.

If you solve what the executive thinks is an AI problem without AI, the executive will still be happy. You can even say, "We were able to solve this without AI using our existing tools and methods. This allowed us to complete the project faster and cheaper than we expected. However, we'll absolutely consider AI for your next problem." The executive will almost always be thrilled you solved the problem, will be willing to give you another one, and you'll develop a good relationship. If you shut the executive down by explaining why they don't know what they are talking about related to AI, they'll probably be hesitant to come to you again.

The same dynamic is at play with any presentation. If people are excited and ready to act on your results, let them get a little carried away with their use of terminology and give them leeway in their layperson's description of how the technical details work (as long as the liberties they are taking won't lead them astray in terms of the actions they'll take). Be happy the audience is on board and ready to act based on your work. If you aren't careful, a desire to ensure technical accuracy across the board can needlessly detract from the success of your presentation.

Note: This tip is based on my blog *The Benefits of Ignoring When Executives Misunderstand Artificial Intelligence* (International Institute For Analytics, January 2019).

Tip 111: Never Pretend You Know If You Don't!

If you're putting together a written document, you can get away with including information that you struggle to understand yourself. For example, perhaps someone on your team provided you with additional technical details on how their portion of a project was executed. Even if you don't understand all the details of that person's work, you can include the information. If questions about your teammate's content come your way after you distribute the document, you can simply direct the questions to the teammate.

In a live presentation, you must be able to explain *everything* you're showing on the screen. If you put a number up on the screen, be able to explain what it is, how it was computed, and why it is relevant. It is all too common for a speaker to refer to a table of data while only being prepared to discuss a small part of the table. If you can't explain the whole table, your choices are to cut out the portions you can't explain, to learn about the parts you can't currently explain, or to have one or more people in the room as backup support (see Tip 97). Don't gamble that nobody will ask a question about the parts you can't explain and expose your ignorance.

Regardless of your preparation level, there are times that your audience will ask a question looking for additional depth or detail that goes beyond your ability to answer, even with your backup experts there for support. That is okay because even the best backup won't be able to handle every question that comes your way.

In the cases when you and your backup experts can't answer, simply state that you aren't the best people to answer at that level of detail, that you know who has the answer, and that you'll follow up later. Having a few occasions when you do have to defer a question that goes too deep can actually win you points with the audience because it shows that you are honest about what you know. Plus, you're the technical expert in the room.

If even you don't know everything, then your largely nontechnical audience feels better about their own lack of knowledge.

What you absolutely can't do is to try and fake that you know more than you do. An audience can see through that very quickly and it will cause them to question everything else you may say. Most readers can probably think of an occasion when a speaker attempted to bluff their way through a question and came off sounding like they had no idea what they were talking about. It is tough to watch as an audience, though ironically the speaker often doesn't realize how they have embarrassed themselves.

Nobody expects you to know every detail about every aspect of a large-scale project. They do, however, expect that in a live presentation you have focused on areas that you are able to readily explain. When they want to dive even deeper than you are prepared to go, they also will respect and appreciate your honesty about your inability to answer on the spot.

Tip 112: Stress the Positive

Just like semantics is everything in politics, semantics matter during a data-driven presentation, especially to a nontechnical audience. Technical people are often straight and to the point with each other. People in nontechnical disciplines may prefer a bit more finesse. Businesspeople, for example, often choose words carefully to make sure that negative, unpopular, or surprising information is received as positively as possible by their own audiences. One approach that helps an audience retain confidence in your results, even in the face of known issues or gaps, is to focus on the positive rather than the negative aspects of what you've found.

For example, suppose that you did initial analysis that only covered the Northeast region. There is no reason to believe the results won't hold elsewhere, but until you run the numbers, you can't say for sure. You could say something like, "We analyzed only the Northeast region, which limits our ability to apply the results more broadly." That sounds negative, and the audience might well decide it isn't worth doing anything until you expand your analysis. A more positive way to say the same thing would be, "Although these results are encouraging and we can take immediate action in the Northeast, we look forward to validating that the results hold for other regions as well." This phrasing emphasizes that you have meaningful results worthy of action today in the Northeast (you do), even though you need to expand and verify them further.

Consider another situation when a major data problem is found. One way to explain it would be, "Given unexpected data issues, we were unable to produce any results for the specialty products category." This raises in the audience's minds the question of what other data issues might exist that would further undercut your findings. It focuses the audience's minds on the negative. A better phrasing would be, "We have high confidence that the results apply to all categories other than the specialty products category. We are in the process of validating if the results hold there as well." In this case, you've made clear that the results apply everywhere with a single exception (that doesn't sound so bad, does it?). You've also expressed that you are on top of determining if the findings also apply to that current exception. The audience will feel comfortable with that.

When delivering your narrative, always apply the lens of how what you say will be heard by the audience. Although you must always be honest, don't shift focus to a few negatives that exist in a sea of positive results. Your audience needs to have confidence in you and your findings, and focusing them on bad news undercuts that confidence by planting seeds of doubt. Even if you plan your talking points well during preparations, it is easy to be too cautious when you are presenting live because the audience makes you more sensitive to what you are saying. Force yourself to stick to what you planned up-front and don't soften your message by letting yourself get intimidated.

In rare cases when most of your findings will be considered bad news, you can still focus on (1) why the results were bad, (2) what can be done to improve the results, and (3) how knowing the bad results can be used to advantage by the audience now that they are aware of the bad results.

Tip 113: Be Honest about Costs as Well as Benefits

It is easy to get excited about your results and focus the audience on the benefits you've found. However, you must also be honest about the costs required to achieve those benefits and the gaps in your findings. This is tough to do and takes discipline when standing in front of a room!

A common mistake occurs when predicting outcomes. Consider a virus that is found in only 0.5% of those tested. We can get 99.5% accuracy rate simply by saying every sample is negative without doing any testing! However, we also would correctly diagnose exactly 0% of those sick. A range of perspectives must be studied including not only true negatives but also false positives, false negatives, and the costs of each.

I once saw someone proudly proclaiming that a model identified over 90% of late payments in advance. Sounds great! The problem? Over 99% of the payments it said would be late were actually on time! In other words, there was a massive false positive rate and each false positive had real costs. Sure, we'd capture 90% of payments that did end up being late, but that doesn't sound quite so compelling once you recognize that for each correctly identified late payment there would be 99 erroneously flagged payments.

Figure 113a illustrates the benefits-focused positioning of a late payment analysis. Figure 113b shows more information and brings the model's flaws into focus. Figure 113c is an appendix with the supporting data showing that although barely 0.5% of payments were late, the model predicted that 40% would be late. Acknowledging the flaws is a critical part of presenting this information.

Our Model Captures 90%+ of Late Payments!

- We can effectively identify late payments 60 days in advance

Total Late Payments Last Year	50k
Late Payments Flagged by Model	46k
Percent of Late Payments Flagged	91%

FIGURE 113A A Misleading Slide Focused Only on the Positive

Our Model Has Serious Flaws

- Although we can identify 90%+ of late payments in advance, only 1% of those we flag as late actually end up being late

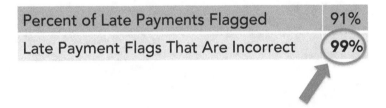

Percent of Late Payments Flagged	91%
Late Payment Flags That Are Incorrect	99%

FIGURE 113B This Slide Draws Attention to a Serious Flaw

Appendix A

- **Following is the detailed data behind our model results**

	Actual		
	Not Late	Late	
Predicted			**Total**
Not Late	6.9M	4,566	**6.9M**
Late	4.5M	46,158	**4.6M**
Total	**11.5M**	**50,724**	

FIGURE 113C The Appendix Provides the Full Picture

Tip 114: Don't Hedge Too Much

We discuss in Tip 113 the need to be honest and to deliver not just positive but also negative findings. A related topic is how much you should hedge your results given the various assumptions and risks that you know apply to the findings. In other words, given a set of results (whether good or bad), there are still a range of assumptions and risks that could serve to enhance or lessen the results. You will often need to discuss these realities as part of delivering a fair and transparent data-driven presentation.

When discussing how well a given investment portfolio would have performed in the past, it is necessary to point out that past performance is no guarantee of future performance. When signing a contract, there is often language discussing that in cases of major natural disaster, war, or civil unrest, either party is able to back out of fulfilling their portion of the contract. In those scenarios, the risks mentioned are standard and nobody worries much about them.

There are also assumptions or risks that are serious and material and those should not be sugarcoated in any way. For example, if I am considering a major surgery and there is a 50% chance I will die, then the doctor must be extremely diligent in explaining that and ensuring that I fully understand it. If I am just having a mole removed, I am still required to sign paperwork acknowledging that all sorts of bad outcomes are possible, but they are rare and neither I nor my doctor spend much time discussing them.

Use that same logic when discussing your effort's risks and assumptions. To the extent that being off just slightly with an assumption is the difference between huge success and huge failure, spend substantial time making that clear. Also spend time on the monitoring and control mechanisms that will be in place to identify and mitigate issues should they arise. In cases when the risks are rare or the assumptions don't have much impact within their plausible ranges, then mention the points to consider, say they aren't high risks, and move on.

I have seen presenters totally destroy the impact and credibility of their presentation by heavily hedging everything they presented. They talk about this risk and that risk. How this assumption may be too high or this assumption may be too low. After hearing enough ways that the results might theoretically be compromised, the audience loses faith in the results and will not act on the information. After too many hedges the audience will decide the findings are unreliable and risky, even if they really aren't.

Most menus will point out that raw seafood can cause illness. People know that and accept it. Imagine, however, that your server starts explaining the percentage of oysters that have some level of contamination, how many people have gotten sick from oysters in the past three months, and the relative illness rates associated with the various oyster varieties available for your dinner. At some point, you become too aware of the risks, and your appetite for oysters disappears.

The restaurant's oysters are no riskier than any other time you've ordered them, but the server's overzealous discussion of the safety risks of the food turns you off. Don't similarly hedge your findings so badly that you turn off your audience.

Tip 115: Be Clear about the Measure You Are Discussing

In the world of analytics, there are many different measures of a predictive model that can be relevant to discuss. Statistical significance is one. Parameter estimates are another. Impacts to the profit and loss statement (P&L) are another. All have merit and add value. What you must do as you discuss such measures is to be very clear about which measure you are discussing at any point in time during your presentation. Even if your slide is labeled, still verbally clarify what you are talking about as you present.

I've heard people discuss what "the most important factors" are in context of each of the three measures listed previously: statistical significance, parameter estimates, or P&L impacts. Although all three measures could lead to such statements, the metrics are very different from each other, and so an ambiguous statement could leave the audience unclear as to which you are referring to. If you don't make crystal clear to the audience what measure you are referring to, then the audience will make their own assumptions . . . and many will be wrong!

In keeping with the goal of influencing your audience, stay away from complex and hard-to-interpret measures. For example, a business audience really doesn't care about parameter estimates directly. What they care about is the impact those parameter estimates imply for their business. Skip technical measures and stick to practical ones. If you talk about how every dollar invested in a campaign will yield two dollars in profit, you'll win them over. If you talk about obscure (to the audience) concepts such as parameter estimates or significance level, you'll be written off as a technical nerd and your impact will be greatly diminished.

Tip 116: Don't Ask Which Findings Are Important

One way to inadvertently detract from your presentation is to ask which findings are important to the audience or, worse, if the findings are important at all. If you don't know that before your presentation, then don't present!

Tips 112, 113, and 114 talk about focusing on the positive and being honest about the negative while not hedging too much. This tip expands on those by suggesting that you never say something to encourage the audience to question if what you've presented is worthwhile to them. If you don't believe your presentation is worthwhile, then don't give it. If you do think it is worthwhile, then assume that your audience agrees and act accordingly.

Although it sounds helpful and open to ask which findings are important or what was valuable in your presentation, remember that you shouldn't ask a question if you aren't prepared to hear the answer. One possible answer to such a question is, "Now that you ask, I am not sure that most of this has any value for me at all!" That answer does not keep you and your audience in a positive mindset.

There are other ways to ask for audience reaction that semantically assume what you said was valuable. For example, instead of asking "Which of these findings are important?" or "Which of these findings are worth acting on?" you could ask "How should we prioritize the actions on these findings?" or "Which finding should we act on first?" The last two questions come from a position of strength that assumes that the findings are valuable. Small adjustments to your semantics as you present can have a major impact on your audience's perception.

Tip 117: Tie Facts to Impacts

Sometimes the relationship between technical facts and a business or practical impact appears obvious. However, you should always make an explicit connection for your audience during your data-driven presentation. As we've discussed many times, the less you make your audience do any heavy lifting, the better. In the end, what the audience really wants most is to understand the impact of your findings. Don't disappoint them!

For example, it sounds great that a credit product enhancement that was just tested will decrease late payments by 10%, but you can't stop there. The audience will also want to know what the dollar impact of that 10% decrease equates to. The math to get from a finding to an impact can be complicated. If you don't do the work for your audience, your presentation will be less successful than it could be. In the worst case, the audience won't bother to do the calculations and they'll fail to take action on your findings because they won't realize the impact they are missing out on.

In another example, your study may identify that a new drug decreases the rate of complications from surgery by 10%. That's obviously good news. What's even better news is to hear how many hospital stays won't be needed, how many deaths are avoided, and how much money per patient will be saved. Anyone in the room will know that the 10% decrease leads to those other positive outcomes, but they won't know the specifics unless you do the computations and then show them.

Figure 117a lists a positive finding but stops short of tying it to broader impacts. Figure 117b adds details on important impacts, which makes the finding far more compelling.

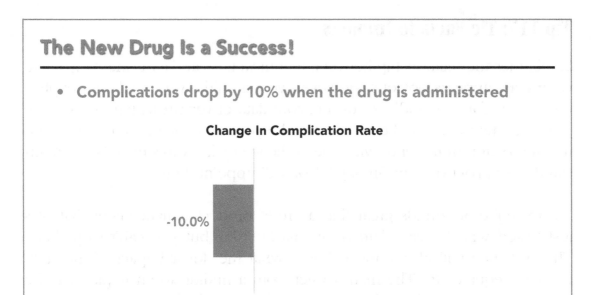

FIGURE 117A A Fact Provided without Associated Impact

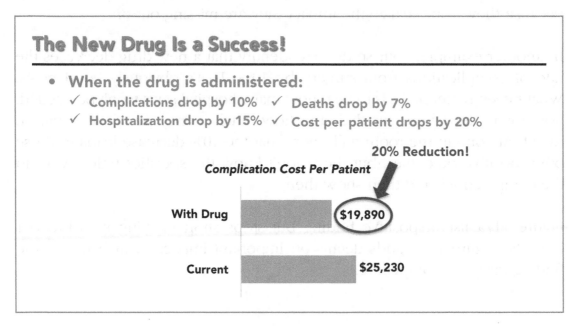

FIGURE 117B Additional Facts Provided along with Impacts

Tip 118: Provide Specific Recommendations for Action

I played soccer for 30 years until my knees couldn't take it anymore and then I shifted to being a referee. I learned a tremendous amount from the senior referee who handled the game assignments for my area. In time, I realized that some of his advice didn't just help me be a better referee but also helped me become a better consultant and presenter.

One of the points the senior referee stressed frequently was that if I was going to make a call during a game, I should do it quickly and with confidence. Good referees trust their judgment and are decisive. I already knew from my playing days that players, coaches, and spectators are able to tell very quickly whether or not a referee is competent and confident. The first few minutes of the game set the tone and, as in other situations, it is hard to change the crowd's first impression.

Once the crowd sees that a referee has confidence and has been making the right calls, they will be much more forgiving when a rare mistake is made because the mistake is clearly the exception. If a referee is visibly struggling with what calls to make, people will feel justified in protesting. Delaying a call is a sign of weakness and indecision, and it isn't possible to command respect while projecting those traits.

This same advice can be applied to data-driven presentations. When asked to present your findings, you should be confident in your work and recommend a path forward for your audience. It starts with confidently presenting and explaining the results you've found and what the results imply as outlined in Tip 117. You must go further, however, by taking a stand and providing specific recommendations for action that will enable the audience to make the potential of what you've found a reality.

Your audience won't always agree with or act on the recommendations that you make. This is no different from spectators believing that a different call should have been made in a game. However, you owe it to your audience to take a stand because they have a lot of other things to worry about. The more you can save the audience from worrying about how to interpret your results by doing it for them, the better.

Figure 118a shows one example of what a recommendations slide might look like. Before this slide, you would have laid out the potential impacts of the actions (see Tip 117). The recommendations are how to make those impacts a reality.

It is your job as the expert to make calls. If you don't have enough confidence in your findings to recommend action, then why should your audience?

> *Note*: This tip is based on content from Chapter 8 of my book *The Analytics Revolution* (Wiley, 2014).

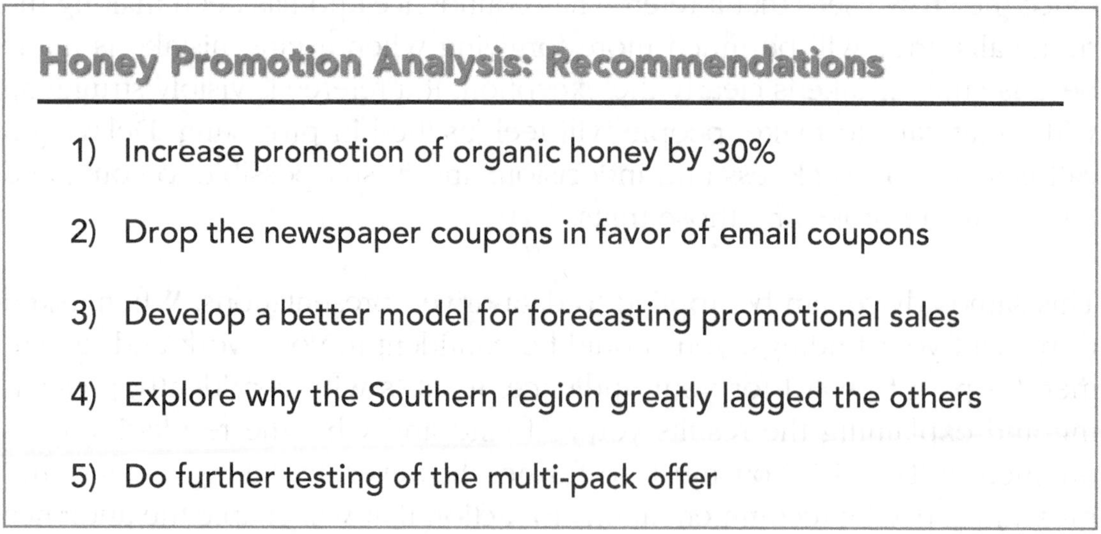

Honey Promotion Analysis: Recommendations

1) Increase promotion of organic honey by 30%

2) Drop the newspaper coupons in favor of email coupons

3) Develop a better model for forecasting promotional sales

4) Explore why the Southern region greatly lagged the others

5) Do further testing of the multi-pack offer

FIGURE 118A Specific Recommendations Provided

Tip 119: Close with a "Wow" Tied to the Larger Context

You put together a terrific data-driven presentation for your audience. You kept your slides clean, short, and visually appealing. You kept the audience focused on just one or two critical pieces of information at a time. You helped them understand what you found and why it is important. You discussed the substantive impacts your findings can facilitate. You even made recommendations that the audience is excited about. Is it time to say thank you and walk off the stage? Not quite.

After your recommendations, the audience is focused narrowly on your specific results. There is usually a significantly larger context within which those results apply. For example, there are critical corporate strategies that are being pursued, long-term goals that must be met, and relationships with customers that must be enhanced. To the extent that you can close your presentation by tying your results to the broader context, you'll get your audience even more motivated to act. Take their mind out of the here-and-now and enable them to place the results in a broader context. Show how following your recommendations will not just help meet the needs of today but will also drive significant progress toward larger goals and strategies over time. Doing so helps end your session with a "wow" moment.

In the honey analysis example we've discussed elsewhere, the audience will certainly be happy to hear the potential impact your recommendations will have on honey sales in the immediate term. Perhaps there is also a corporate strategy to increase presence in the organic honey space. Another corporate strategy is to pursue direct interaction with customers instead of traditional mass marketing. The recommendations from Tip 118 directly support both strategies. Whatever short-term benefits the audience will experience by following your advice, the bonus you can offer is that they will also be taking actions that align with longer-term strategies and priorities. Supporting the broader strategies and priorities is a great path to getting promoted and long-term success, so audience members will be even more motivated to act once they leave the room.

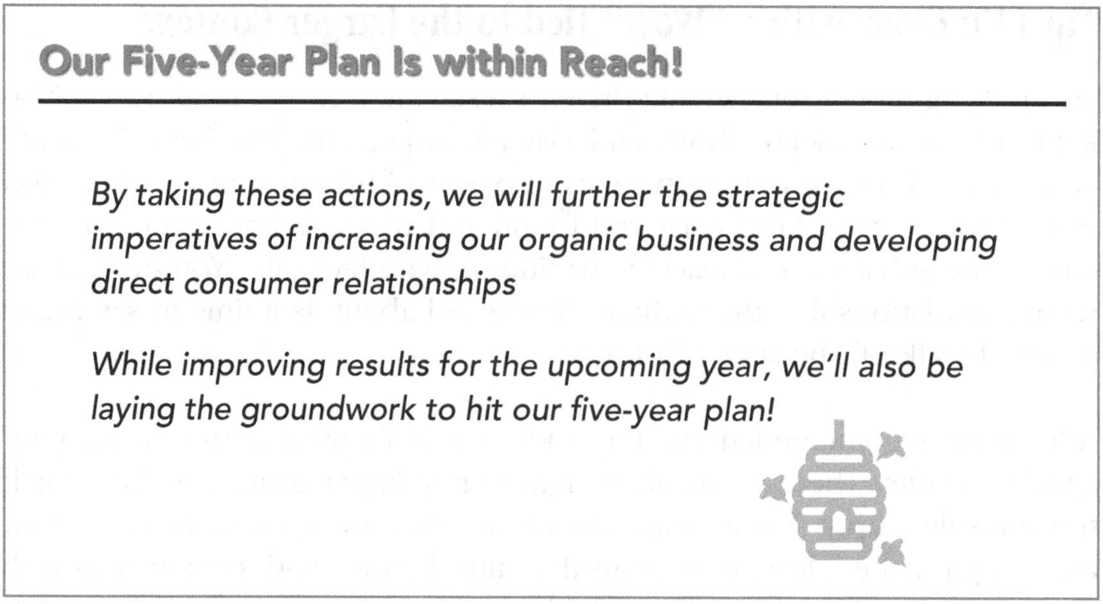

Our Five-Year Plan Is within Reach!

By taking these actions, we will further the strategic imperatives of increasing our organic business and developing direct consumer relationships

While improving results for the upcoming year, we'll also be laying the groundwork to hit our five-year plan!

FIGURE 119A Results Tied to the Larger Context

Figure 119a has an example of how to tie our honey analysis into a bigger context. It shows that today's results have long-term, strategic importance that go beyond the tactical benefits of today.

Closing with a tie to the larger context can put a "wow" lens on top of your findings. Whether you have a short slide for this final appeal or you just verbalize it, it is a terrific way to end your presentation with a bang.

Afterword

Winning the Room is a comprehensive guide for everyone seeking maximum impact and audience engagement from their presentations. Bill Franks reflects on his own journey and learnings from decades of presenting, showcasing what worked well and what should be avoided. And he does an outstanding job making it tangible, sharing his experience and providing many examples and illustrations, which makes for a hands-on, pragmatic, and also entertaining read.

Franks provides well over 100 pertinent tips and tricks on how to best convey insights, how to tell an engaging story, and how to connect with an audience. From planning a presentation, its design, and storyboard; to choosing the appropriate level of detail to be conveyed; and closing with advice on optimal presentation delivery; *Winning the Room* covers it all.

The author draws from his rich history as an educator, researcher, and chief analytics officer as he places special attention on one critical skill that's regularly at the heart of successful presentations: the translation of data into charts, figures, and, ultimately, credible insights. Readers will learn how to sidestep the common pitfalls of poor data representation and learn specific actions to take to increase the likelihood that an audience will be able to follow and understand a presentation even of complex datasets and challenging insights.

Winning the Room is relevant to a broad audience: The book is a pointed refresher for more-seasoned business leaders, project managers, researchers, and consultants. It's also the one complete reference on presentation preparation for those early in their career: professionals, academics, and students alike. It's a wonderful reminder of how optimal presentation preparation creates a platform to elevate solid work into something impactful and consequential, and of how, conversely, even the best ideas, findings, and analyses will suffer diminished returns and lessened relevancy when presentation preparation is incomplete or an afterthought only.

Bill Franks penned a strikingly germane and practical handbook on how to connect and resonate with a presentation audience. His advice is highly relevant and applicable in virtual as well as in-person presentation settings and adds a seasoned practitioner's perspective on how to create results, not just reports.

Rasmus Wegener, PhD
Senior partner, Bain & Company

About the Author

Bill Franks is the director of the Center for Statistics and Analytical Research at Kennesaw State University. He is also chief analytics officer for The International Institute For Analytics (IIA) and serves on several corporate advisory boards. Franks is the author of the books *Taming the Big Data Tidal Wave*, *The Analytics Revolution*, and *97 Things about Ethics Everyone in Data Science Should Know*. He is a sought-after speaker and frequent blogger who has over the years been ranked a top global big data influencer, a top global artificial intelligence (AI) and big data influencer, a top AI influencer, and was an inaugural inductee into the Analytics Hall of Fame. Including several years as chief analytics officer for Teradata (NYSE: TDC), he has worked with clients in a variety of industries for companies ranging in size from Fortune 100 companies to small nonprofit organizations. You can learn more at http://www.bill-franks.com.

About the Website

Thank you for purchasing this book.

You may access the following additional complementary bonus resources provided for your use by visiting:

URL: www.wiley.com\go\Franks\WinningtheRoom

Password: Franks123

At this link, you will find color versions of all the illustrations in the book. To keep the price of the book as low as possible, the print version is in black and white. The web content is a way to allow those with a paper copy to still see the full-color versions of the book's illustrations. While the electronic versions of the book are already in color, the web content allows those with an electronic copy of the book to see the illustrations in a larger format. We do hope that you enjoy both the book and the bonus content!

Index

Page numbers followed by *f* refer to figures.

Abbreviations, 118, 119*f*
Academic presentations, 28
Accent graphics, 159, 160*f*
Accuracy
    double-checking, 126, 127*f*
    precision and, 103, 104*f*
Acronyms, 118, 119*f*
Actions, recommended. *see* Recommended
    actions
Action Settings feature, in PowerPoint, 50–51,
    51*f,* 209
Advance copies, of presentation, 210–211
Advertising, mass, 4
Agenda items
    addressing all, 87, 88*f*
    identifying coverage of, 89, 90*f*
Agenda slides, 87, 88*f,* 89, 90*f*
Aggregations, 122, 123*f*
"All Other" category, 167, 168*f*
Analogies, 37
Animations
    highlighting numbers with, 202
    slide timing with, 185
    using, 48, 49*f*
Appendices
    and action settings, 50
    to clarify illustrations, 198
    costs and benefits in, 236, 238*f*
    and definition slides, 120
    as leave-behind documents, 38, 39*f*

Architectural diagrams, 157, 158*f*
Arrows, 198, 199*f*
Assumptions, presenting, 239–240
Audience(s)
    addressing concerns of, 217–218
    adjusting story to, 182–184, 183*f*
    asking questions of, 194, 242
    building trust with, 24
    color-blind, 153
    correcting your, 230–231
    cutting content and confusing, 190–191
    difficult, 228–229
    eye contact with. *see* Eye contact
    headlines for, 56–57
    informing, of ethical concerns, 196, 197*f*
    keeping attention of, 16
    knowing your, 12–13
    managing, 59
    presenting complex analyses to, 4
    providing details to, 33–34
    response of, to text-dense slides, 8
    scaling figures for, 192
    technical diagrams for, 157, 158*f*
Authenticity, 23
Average, 200, 201*f*
Axis labeling
    for cause-and-effect relationships, 173,
        173*f,* 174*f*
    clarifying aggregations in, 123*f*
    and data labels, 169, 170
    starting point for, 132, 133*f*
Axis range, 132

Background colors, 153
Backup data, 7
Backup plans, 207–208
Bad news, delivering, 235
Bar charts
    data labels for, 169, 169f, 170f
    ease of interpreting, 147
    stacked, 171–172, 171f–172f
Being yourself, 23
Benefits-focused positioning, 236, 237f
Body language, 223–224
Bold fonts
    consistent use of, 82
    highlighting numbers with, 202, 203f
    highlighting text with, 204, 205f
    shading and, 163, 164f
Borders, chart, 165, 166f
Bright lighting, 222
Bullet points, 80, 181
Business context, presenting, 54–55
Business presentations, 27

Camera, looking at, 225, 226f
Categories
    "All Other," 167, 168f
    naming, 114, 115f
    number of, 167, 168f
    in stacked bar charts, 171
Cause-and-effect relationships, 173–174, 173f,
        174f
Chart(s). See also Graphics
    bar, 147, 169, 171, 171f–172f, 172
    borders in, 165, 166f
    for cause-and-effect relationships, 173–174,
        173f, 174f
    color coordination, 153–154, 154f
    comprehensible. see Comprehensible
        charts
    data labels in, 169–170, 169f–170f
    easy-to-interpret, 147–148
    formats of, 145–148, 148f
    highlighting numbers in, 202
    line, 147

pie, 167, 168f
raw output in, 142–144
scale in. see Scale and scaling
scientific notation in, 112
simplicity of, 145, 146f
with spelling and grammatical
        errors, 93, 93f
stacked bar, 171, 171f–172f, 172
variety in type of, 137, 138f
Churn modeling, 124
Clarification
    of acronyms and abbreviations,
        118, 119f
    with definitions, 70, 71f
    of results, 35–36
Clarity
    about implications of results, 194–195
    about measures used, 241
    of charts and graphs, 16
Clean layout, 15f
Coaches, inside, 180
Colors
    background, 153
    context for, 155–156, 155f–156f
Color-blind audiences, 153
Color coordination
    in charts, 153–154, 154f
    highlighting numbers with, 202, 203f
    for important texts, 204, 205f
    for readable texts, 163, 164f
Columns, 99, 163
Comma separators, for numbers, 105,
        106f–107f
Commentary, verbal, 9, 14, 215–216
Comparison slides, precision in, 101,
        101f–102f, 102
Complex analysis, presenting, 4
Complex dashboards, 45, 46f–47f
Complex graphics, 151, 152f
Complex issues, analogies for, 37
Comprehensible charts
    format of, 147, 148, 148f
    importance of, 16–17, 149, 150f

labels for, 72–73
simplicity of, 145, 146*f*
Conference presentations, 27–28
Confidants, consulting, 13, 179–180
Confidence
    positivity to build, 234, 235
    precision and, 103, 104*f*
    in recommended actions, 245–246
Confidence monitors, 219
Confidentiality notices, 211
Confusion
    about implication of results, 194–195
    cutting content without creating, 190–191
Consistency
    in font, 82, 83, 83*f*, 84*f*
    in formatting, 161, 162*f*
    in phrasing, 74, 75*f*
    in precision level, 99–100, 99*f*, 100*f*
    in scale, 130, 131*f*
Consultations, with confidants, 179–180
Content
    breaking up, 45, 46*f*, 47*f*
    cutting, 18, 187–191
    slide, 14
Contentious points, 29, 59
Context
    business and practical, 54–55
    for color choice, 155–156, 155*f*–156*f*
    providing, verbally, 14
    for results, 247–248, 248*f*
Controversial points, 29, 59
Copyright notice, 76, 211
Costs, honesty about, 236, 237*f*–238*f*
Credibility, building
    with accurate data, 126
    by addressing agenda items, 87
    backup support for, 206
    with charts and graphs, 16
    by clarifying aggregations, 122
    with comprehensible numbers, 240
    importance of, 24
    by keeping colors in context, 155
    and sending advance copies, 210

and spelling/grammatical errors, 91
with technical details, 91
and truncated labels, 116
Critical numbers, 202, 203*f*, 221
Cutting and pasting, inconsistent fonts from, 83*f*

Dashboards, 45, 46*f*–47*f*
Data
    backup, 7
    business vs. practical context for, 54–55
    relevant, 52–53
Data-dense slides, 52, 53*f*
Data labels
    and axis starting point, 132, 133*f*
    use of, 169–170, 169*f*–170*f*
Data literacy, 5–6
Decimals, numbers with, 108, 109*f*
Decision trees, 151, 152*f*
Default font, 85
Definitions
    clarifying, 70, 71*f*
    dedicated slides for, 120, 121*f*
    simple, 67–68
Delivery, 213–248
    addressing audience's concerns, 217–218
    anticipating random and irrelevant questions, 227
    asking questions of audience, 242
    clarity about measures used, 241
    context for results, 247, 248, 248*f*
    correcting people, 230–231
    eye contact in, 219–220
    handling difficult people, 228–229
    hedging results, 239–240
    honesty during, 236, 237*f*–238*f*
    and lighting, 222
    movement in, 223–224
    for online presentations, 225, 226*f*
    pointing to important information, 221
    positive language in, 234–235

Delivery (*Continued*)
  questions you can't answer, 232–233
  reading slides, 215–216
  recommendations for action, 245–246, 246*f*
  tying facts to impact, 243, 244*f*
Design, 25–61
  analogies, 37
  animations, 48–49
  appendices, 38, 39*f*
  and business vs. practical context for
      data, 54–55
  and content delivery, 45–47
  headlines, 56–57
  of launch slides, 43–44
  of leave-behind documents, 40–42
  organizational strategies, 29–30
  PowerPoint action settings, 50–51
  recommended actions, 58–59
  relevant data in, 52–53
  requests for clarification, 35–36
  technical details, 31–34
  venue-based, 27–28
  "why" aspect of presentation, 60–61
Details
  attention to, 122
  excessive, 31–32
  quantity of, 33–34
  technical, 31–34, 151, 177, 232
Diagrams
  architectural, 157, 158*f*
  technical, 157, 158*f*
Distractions, 52
Diverse audiences, 184
Documents, leave-behind, 38, 39*f*,
      40–42, 41*f*
Due dates, 22
Dykes, Brent, 182

Easy-to-interpret charts, 147–148, 148*f*
Easy-to-read fonts, 82
Effective Data Storytelling (Dykes), 182
Elevator pitches, 187

Errors
  grammatical, 91–94, 92*f*, 93*f*
  spelling, 91–94, 92*f*, 93*f*
  word substitution, 94, 94*f*
Ethical concerns, 196, 197*f*
Excel
  axis labeling in, 132
  scale of graphs in, 130
Executive presentations, 20–21
Eye contact
  with bright lighting, 222
  and looking at the screen, 219–220
  in online presentations, 224, 225*f*

Facts
  focusing on figures and, 10–11
  tying, to impacts, 243, 244*f*
Feedback, 179–180
Figures. *See also* Numbers
  focusing on facts and, 10–11
  relatable scale for, 192, 193*f*
Finance, audiences in, 183
Font(s). *See also* Bold fonts
  consistent, 82, 83, 83*f*–84*f*
  default, 85
  easy-to-read, 82
  italic, 82, 204, 205*f*
  missing, 85–86, 86*f*
  unusual, 145
Font size
  choosing, 78, 79*f*
  for large tables, 163
  making numbers stand out with,
      202, 203*f*
Footnotes, 118, 119*f*
Formats and formatting
  chart, 145–148, 148*f*
  number, 105, 106*f*–107*f*
  table, 161, 162*f*

Gradients, 145
Grammar checking software, 91–94, 92*f*

Grammatical errors, 91–94, 92*f,* 93*f*
Graphs
    comprehensible, 16–17
    raw numbers in, 105, 108
    scientific notation in, 112
    spelling and grammatical errors, 93*f*
    truncated labels in, 116
Graphics. *See also* Chart(s)
    accent, 159, 160*f*
    borders for, 165, 166*f*
    color coordination for, 153, 154, 154*f*
    complex, 151, 152*f*
    context of colors in, 155, 155*f*–156*f,* 156
    data labels for, 169, 169*f*–170*f,* 170
    illustrations, 198, 199*f*
    incomprehensible, 149, 150*f*
    number of categories in, 167, 168*f*
    spelling and grammatical errors in, 93
    technical and architectural dia-
        grams, 157, 158*f*

Headers, 89, 90*f*
Headlines, 56–57
Hedging results, 239–240
High-level summary of concepts, 43
Highlighting information
    with animations, 49*f*
    by pointing, 221
    in tables and charts, 202, 203*f*
Honesty
    about costs and benefits, 236, 237*f*–238*f*
    about questions you can't answer,
        232, 233
Horizontal text, 95, 96*f*
Hyperlinks, 50, 51*f*

Illustrations, simplified, 198, 199*f*
Images. *see* Graphics
Impact
    closing with "wow" moment, 247–248
    and level of detail, 31–32
    tying facts to, 243, 244*f*

Important information
    asking audience to identify, 242
    highlighting text containing,
        204, 205*f*
    pointing to, in presentation, 221
Information
    about audience, 12
    in appendices, 38
    data literacy as delivering, 5–6
    highlighting, 49*f,* 202, 203*f,* 221
    important, 204, 205*f,* 221, 242
    low-value, 200, 201*f*
    targeting specific pieces of, 45, 46*f*
Information technology, audiences
    in, 157
Inside coaches, 180
Interactive webinars, 50
Interest rates, displaying, 108
Interpretation, ease of, 147–148
Introduction, developing your, 56–57
Irrelevant questions, anticipating, 227
Italic font, 82, 204, 205*f*

Labels
    acronyms and abbreviations in,
        118–119, 119*f*
    for agenda-related content, 89, 90*f*
    axis, 123*f,* 132, 133*f,* 169, 170
    comprehensible, 72–73
    data, 132, 133*f,* 169–170, 169*f*–170*f*
    and definition slides, 120–121
    identifying aggregations in, 122–123
    for outcome of interest, 124–125
    and scale in charts, 128–131
    slanted, 95, 96*f*
    system, 72, 73*f*
    truncated, 116
    value, 169
Launch slides, 43–44, 44*f*
Layouts, slide
    clean and visual, 14–15, 15*f*
    mixing, 139, 140*f*–141*f*

Layperson terms
    labels in, 72
    using, 67–68, 68f
Leave-behind documents
    appendices as, 38, 39f
    creating, 40–42, 41f
Lighting, 222
Lines, in tables, 163, 164f
Line charts
    data labels on, 169, 169f, 170f
    ease of interpreting, 147
Line spacing, for text, 80, 80f, 81f
Literacy, 5
Long presentations, 18–19
Low-value information, 200, 201f

Machine learning models, 198
Marketing, audiences in, 183
Mass advertising, 4
Measures
    clarity about, 241
    relative, 198
    statistical, 128
Metrics, colors for, 155–156, 155f–156f
Microsoft 365 Powerpoint
    Action Settings in, 50–51, 51f
    applying consistent color palette, 153–154,
        153f, 154f
    numbering slides, 134, 134f
    printing notes pages, 40, 41f–42f
Mindset, of audience, 217–218
Missing fonts, 85–86, 86f
Misspelled words, 91–94, 92f, 93f
Model performance, terms for, 67f–68f
Movement, during delivery, 223–224
Multicolor gradients, 145

Names, category, 114, 115f
Narrative. see Story
News, bad, 235
Non-horizontal texts, 95, 96f
Notes pages, 40, 41f–42f

Numbers
    accuracy of, 103–104, 126–127
    as category designations, 114–115
    critical, 202, 203f
    displaying percentages as, 108–109
    double-checking accuracy of,
        126–127
    formatting, 105, 106f–107f
    noting differences in, 200, 201f
    precision of, 99–104
    quantities and percentages for, 110–111
    raw, 105, 108
    scientific notation for, 112–113
    slide, 134

Off-topic discussions, 227
Online presentations
    eye contact for, 225, 226f
    movement in, 224
Order, of slides, 29–30
Organizational strategies
    ordering content, 29–30
    starting with recommended actions, 58
    using headlines, 56–57
Outcome(s)
    asking audience to identify
        important, 242
    focusing on outcome of interest,
        124, 125f
    predicting, 236
Outlines, 56
Outputs, raw, 142, 143f–144f
Overpreparation, 181

Paragraph spacing, 80
Parameter estimates (measure), 241
PDF format, 85
Percentages
    accuracy of, 103
    displaying, 108, 109f
    providing quantities and, 110, 111f
% symbol, 108

Performance, terms for, 67*f*–68*f*
Phrasing
  consistent, 74, 75*f*
  positive, 234–235
Pie charts, 167, 168*f*
Plain language, 118
P&L impacts (measure), 241
Pointers, in online meeting systems, 221
Pointing to important information, 221
Points on graphs, labels for, 169
Positive phrasing, 234–235
PowerPoint
  Action Settings feature, 50–51, 51*f,* 209
  axis labeling in, 132
  color palettes in, 153
  default fonts in, 85
  inserting slide numbers in, 134, 134*f*
  line spacing in, 80–81
  printing notes section in, 40, 41*f*–42*f*
  printing out slides in, 188–189, 188*f*–189*f*
  scaling graphs in, 130
Practical context, for data, 54–55
Practice presentations, 177–178
Precision
  consistency in level of, 99–100, 99*f,* 100*f*
  in delivery of presentation, 194, 195
  level of accuracy and, 103, 104*f*
  necessary level of, 101–102, 101*f*–102*f*
Preparation, 175–211
  adjusting story to audience, 182–184, 183*f*
  backup support, 206
  budgeting time for, 22
  clarifying implications of results, 194–195
  consulting confidants, 179–180
  creating backup plans, 207–208
  cutting content, 187–191
  highlighting critical numbers, 202, 203*f*
  highlighting important text, 204, 205*f*
  informing audience of ethical concerns, 196, 197*f*
  for long vs. short presentations, 18–19
  overpreparation, 181
  practice, 177–178
  removing low-value information, 200, 201*f*
  scaling figures, 192, 193*f*
  sending advance copies, 210–211
  shortening presentations, 187–189
  simplified illustrations, 198, 199*f*
  slide clickers, 209
  time limits, 185, 186*f*
Presentation(s)
  academic, 28
  business, 27
  conference, 27–28
  executive, 20–21
  online, 224, 225, 226*f*
  for project success, 3–4
  recorded, 223–224
  short vs. long, 18–19
Presentation style, 23
Printouts
  for executive presentations, 21*f*
  of notes section, 40, 41*f*–42*f*
  of slides, 188–189, 188*f*–189*f*
Problem solving, 231
Process launch slides, 44*f*
Proofreading, 94

Quantities, providing percentages and, 110, 111*f*
Questions
  about business significance, 54
  anticipating random and irrelevant, 227
  asking your audience, 194, 242
  passing, to experts, 206
  setting aside time for, 187
  that you can't answer, 232–233

Random questions, anticipating, 227
Raw numbers, 105, 108
Raw outputs, 142, 143*f*–144*f*
Readable text, 76, 77*f*

Recommended actions
   presenting, with confidence,
      245–246, 246*f*
   starting presentations with, 58–59
   technical details vs., 32
Recorded presentations, 223–224
Redundancy, reducing, 177
Relatable figures, 192, 193*f*
Relative measures, 198
Repetition, 139
Reports, written, 28, 40, 198
Response model evaluation, terms for, 67
Results
   accurate, 3
   clarifying implications of, 194–195
   discussing how to use, 35–36
   hedging, 239–240
   and project success, 3–4
   relevance of, 54
   scale for, 192
   summarizing, 32
Right word, wrong place errors, 94, 94*f*
Risks, presenting, 239–240

SAS (statistical package), 142, 143*f*–144*f*
Scale and scaling
   consistent, 130, 131*f*
   relatable, 192, 193*f*
   use of, 128, 129*f*
Scatterplots, 173–174
Scientific notation, 112, 113*f*
Screen
   looking at, 219–220
   reading from, 215–216
Script, using, 181
Section breaks, 89, 90*f*
Self-awareness, of delivery style, 23
Semantics, 38, 234
Senior executives, 20–21
Shading, in tables, 163, 164*f*
Short presentations, 18–19, 187–189
Short slides, 14–15

Simplifying
   charts, 145, 146*f*
   illustrations, 198, 199*f*
   technical terms, 67–68, 67*f,* 68*f*
Slang, 118
Slanted labels, 95, 96*f*
Slide(s). *See also* Layouts, slide
   agenda, 87, 88*f,* 89, 90*f*
   animations on, 48–49
   comparison, 101, 101*f*–102*f,* 102
   controlling your, 209
   data-dense, 52, 53*f*
   definition, 120, 121*f*
   effective, 14–15
   for executive presentations, 20–21
   launch, 43, 44*f*
   order of, 29–30
   printouts of, 21*f,* 188–189, 188*f*–189*f*
   quantity of, 185, 186*f*
   reading from, 215–216
   recommendations, 246, 246*f*
   salient points on, 9, 9*f*
   short, 14–15
   text-dense, 7–9
Slide clickers, 209
Slide-free presentations, 20–21
Slide master, 50
Slide numbers, 134, 134*f*
Software packages, technical, 142, 142*f*–144*f*
"So what" aspect of presentation, 60, 61*f*
Spacing, of text, 80, 80*f*–81*f*
Spell checking software, 91–94, 92*f*
Spelling errors, 91–94, 92*f,* 93*f*
Stacked bar charts, 171–172, 171*f*–172*f*
Statistical measures, 128
Statistical packages, 142, 143*f*–144*f*
Statistical significance (measure), 241
Story
   adjusting, to audience, 182–184, 183*f*
   defined, 10
   developing your, 7, 8–9, 8*f,* 10–11
   flow of, 29*f,* 30*f*

Strategic fundamentals, 1–24
  being yourself, 23
  budgeting time for preparation, 22
  building trust with audience, 24
  comprehensible charts and graphs,
    16–17
  data literacy, 5–6
  effective slides, 14–15
  executive presentations, 20–21
  facts and figures, 10–11
  knowing your audience, 12–13
  results and project success, 3–4
  short vs. long presentations, 18–19
  text-dense slides, 7–9
Summarizing concepts, 43
Support, 206
Supporting text, 76, 77*f*
System labels, 72, 73*f*

Tables, 169
  font size for, 163
  formatting, 161, 162*f*
  highlighting numbers in, 202
  raw numbers/output in, 105, 108, 142
  shading in, 163, 164*f*
  truncated labels in, 116, 116*f*
  understanding parts of, 232
Technical detail(s)
  appropriate level of, 33–34
  in complex graphics, 151
  impact and level of, 31–32
  questions you can't answer
    about, 232
  rehearsing to adjust level of, 177
Technical diagrams, 157–158
Technical software packages, output from,
  142, 142*f*–144*f*
Technical terms
  abbreviations and acronyms for, 118
  avoiding, 69
  simplifying, 67–68, 67*f*, 68*f*
Templates, spacing in, 80

Text
  on charts and images, 93
  consistent fonts for, 82–83, 83*f*–84*f*
  font size, 78, 79*f*
  horizontal, 95, 96*f*
  important, 204, 205*f*
  in labels, 72–73
  missing fonts for, 85–86
  quantity of, 65, 66*f*, 78, 79*f*
  readable, 76, 77*f*
  spacing in, 80, 80*f*–81*f*
  spelling and grammar errors in, 91–92
  supporting, 76, 77*f*
  underlined, 204, 205*f*
Text-dense slides, 7–9
97 Things about Ethics Everyone in
    Data Science Should Know
    (Franks), 196
3D features, 145
Time, for preparation, 22
Time limits, 18, 185–187, 186*f*
Timing, practicing to gauge, 177
Transparent animations, 48, 49*f*
Truncated labels, 116, 116*f*–117*f*
Trust building, 24
Typos, 93

Underlined text, 204, 205*f*

Value labels, 169
Venue, adapting design to, 27–28
Verbal commentary, 9, 14, 215–216
Video recordings, 178, 223–224
Vision, presenting your, 11
Visual slide layouts, 14–15, 15*f*

Webinars, interactive, 50
"What" aspect of presentation, 60, 61*f*
"What now" aspect of presentation,
    60, 61*f*
"Why" aspect of presentation, 60–61
Wiley, 5

Words and wording
  for agenda items, 87–90
  and consistent phrasing, 74, 75*f*
  definitions, 67–68, 70, 71*f*
  positive, 234–235
  quantity of, 65, 66*f,* 78, 79*f*
  spelling and grammatical errors, 91–92
  technical terms, 67–69

Word substitution errors, 94, 94*f*
"Wow" moment, 247–248
Wrap-up section, 50
Written reports, 28, 40, 198

x-axis, 173, 173*f*–174*f*

y-axis, 173, 173*f*–174*f*